YOUR SEVEN
ENERGY
CENTERS

YOUR SEVEN
ENERGY
CENTERS

*A Holistic Approach
to Physical, Emotional and
Spiritual Vitality*

ELIZABETH CLARE PROPHET
AND PATRICIA R. SPADARO

SUMMIT UNIVERSITY PRESS
Corwin Springs, Montana

YOUR SEVEN ENERGY CENTERS
A Holistic Approach to Physical, Emotional and Spiritual Vitality
by Elizabeth Clare Prophet and Patricia R. Spadaro
Copyright © 2000 by Summit University Press
All rights reserved

Library of Congress Catalog Card Number: 00-101825
ISBN: 0-922729-56-5

SUMMIT UNIVERSITY 🕊 PRESS
Summit University Press and 🕊 are registered trademarks.

Printed in the United States of America
06 05 04 03 02   7 6 5 4 3

Contents

CONTENTS

Note: Because gender-neutral language can be cumbersome and at times confusing, we have often used *he* and *him* to refer to God or the individual and *man* to refer to people in general. These terms are for readability only and are not intended to exclude women or the feminine aspect of the Godhead. Likewise, our use of the term *God* or *Spirit* is not meant to exclude other expressions for the Divine.

Integrating Body, Mind and Spirit

The human body is only
vitality, energy, and spirit....
If you want to learn the Great Way,
you must value the three treasures.
                                    —LÜ YEN

Vitality. Everybody wants it, but in today's complex and stressful world few of us know how to capture it—and keep it. That's because real vitality is more than a matter of good sleep, vitamins and pumping iron. Real vitality is physical, emotional *and* spiritual.

Vitality comes from understanding your most important natural resource—energy. It comes from knowing how to tap into your energy source. How to clear the blocks to making that connection.

How to master the flow of energy so you can express your full potential.

The ancient wisdom of the world's spiritual traditions has much to teach us about the science of vitalizing body, mind and soul. Again and again these traditions talk about seven levels of being and seven centers for the exchange of energy from the spiritual world to our world.

The seven heavens of Judaism, the seven tiers of Kabbalah's Tree of Life,[1] Christianity's seven sacraments, and the seven chakras of Hinduism and Buddhism—they are all ways of describing how we can tap into higher levels of spiritual awareness to accelerate the flow of energy from Spirit to matter, from heaven to earth, from within to without.

In this book, our starting point is the ancient Eastern science of the body's seven energy centers, or chakras. The network of the chakras forms a road map that can help you explore your physical, emotional and spiritual worlds. For there is much more to you—and to your vitality—than meets the eye.

Coordinates of Spirit

Our energy centers operate at subtle levels, invisible to the physical eye. Yet they affect every aspect of our life, including our vitality, our creativity and our well-being.

In simple terms, you can think of the energy centers as receiving- and sending-stations for the energy that flows to you, through you and out from you moment by moment. Each center is like a step-down transformer that translates this powerful energy from Spirit to a different level of our being, nourishing body, mind and soul. Each one has a unique part to play in the process of daily living and spiritual growth.

The seven major energy centers are situated at etheric levels of our being along the spinal column at the base of the spine, midway between the base and the navel, at the navel, the heart, the throat, the brow and the top of the head.[2] We have all experienced energy flowing through our seven chakras, whether we have realized it or not.

The energy of the base-of-the-spine chakra enables us to connect with the earth and nature and to stay grounded and practical as we master the day-to-day, physical level of existence. Along with the seat-of-the-soul chakra, it governs our sexuality. Through the seat-of-the-soul chakra, we also receive our gut reactions and hunches and we liberate our soul to fulfill her life plan. Through the solar-plexus chakra, our center of peace, we express and master our emotions and desires.

Our heart center inspires us with the compassion and generosity to be love in action. Through the throat center, we have access to the tremendous power of will and the spoken word to create personal and world change. Our third-eye center enables us to focus, see a situation clearly and tap into the highest truth. And through the crown chakra, we engage our intellect, receive those sudden flashes of illumination and experience enlightenment.

The chakras are points of contact with dimensions of our being beyond the physical, and yet they mesh with the physical. They are coordinates, so to speak, of Spirit right within our own bodies.

The idea that the spiritual world is mirrored in the material world and in our own physical body is an ancient one. "As is the atom, so is the universe," say the Upanishads. "Within the pulp of a millet seed an entire universe can be found.... In the pupil of the eye, an endless heaven," writes Sufi poet Mahmud Shabestari. And the famous Hermetic axiom states, "As is the great, so is the small; as it is above, so it is below." In other words, the pattern of Spirit is indelibly imprinted within the very fabric of our being.

The world's sages and healers tell us that as a result of our inner resonance with the divine, the power to heal ultimately comes from within ourselves. Twentieth-century seer and healer Edgar Cayce, for instance, taught that all healing comes from "attuning each atom of the body, each reflex of the brain forces, to the awareness of the divine" that lies within each atom and cell of the body. He also said that true healing can only take place once there is an awakening of the spiritual self.

What lies behind us and what lies before us are tiny matters compared to what lies within us.

—RALPH WALDO EMERSON

Our body's seven energy centers are the gateways to that spiritual self. When we understand how these centers work, we can work with them to bring our body, mind and emotions back into balance with our true nature.

Wheels of Life

The word *chakra* is Sanskrit for "wheel" or "disc." Each chakra is symbolically depicted as a lotus that has a different number of petals. The more petals the chakra has, the higher its frequency or vibration. The ancient sages taught that the primal spiritual life-force (known as the Kundalini) is sealed within the chakra that is located at the base of the spine.

We can unlock that powerful latent energy through acts of love, service to life, meditation and prayer. As the Kundalini rises along the spine, it activates each chakra along the way and causes the "wheel" to spin, the "lotus" to blossom.

The seventh energy center, the crown chakra, is known as the thousand-petaled lotus. When this center is fully opened, we reach what the Buddhists call enlightenment. Statues and thankas depict the Buddhas, who have reached this stage, with an aura of fire around their form and a flame-like protuberance springing from the top of their heads. Christian artists portray this attainment as a golden halo encircling the heads of the holy ones.

As each energy center "spins," it emanates its own unique frequency and color that keys into one of the seven rainbow rays of light. If we could see ourselves at spiritual levels, however, we would see that the light emanating from each chakra varies in its intensity and purity, depending on whether the energy flowing through the channel of our chakras is balanced or blocked. The stronger and more pure emanations indicate a strong and balanced flow of energy. The weaker and duller emanations indicate a blocked flow of energy at that chakra.

When an energy center is blocked, we can experience fatigue or health problems, emotional imbalances and lethargy. When energy is flowing freely through an energy center, we feel energetic, creative and at peace.

The Science of Energy Flow

All of life is energy. The mystics even defined God as light, as energy and as the flow of that light and energy.* The first letter of John in the New Testament proclaimed that "God is light." "In each atom," said Shabestari, "lies the blazing light of a thousand suns." And in the Tao Te Ching, the Chinese sage Lao Tzu teaches, "Something mysteriously

---

*Some traditions call this energy *ch'i* or *prana.*

formed, born before heaven and earth. . . . Ever present and in motion. . . . I do not know its name. Call it Tao. For lack of a better word, I call it great. Being great, it flows. It flows far away. Having gone far, it returns."[3]

For Lao Tzu, the definition of the Universal Spirit was flow, movement. Life coursing through our veins, our minds, our hearts is energy, is movement, is God. Lao Tzu also tells us that there is a natural order to the universe and to our own lives, and when we work against that natural order we create inharmony and unhappiness.

The choice is ours. At every moment the crystal clear stream of life descends to us from our Source in its natural rhythm. This energy is distributed first to our heart center and then to our other chakras. It is the life-force that beats our heart, gives us the impetus to grow and evolve, and energizes the organs and systems of our body.

But we always have free will. We can express this energy in a positive way or we can upset the natural flow by acting out of sync with our spiritual nature. We can, for instance, use the energy of our heart center to be naturally kind, loving and charitable, or we can use it to be selfish and stingy.

We can express the power of our throat center through communication that is caring or critical.

These choices have consequences. When we use energy to think, feel or act in ways that are positive, we attract to ourselves more of that positive energy, as if we were priming the pump. When we mold that energy in ways that are not true to our inner nature, we create mental and emotional toxins that block energy flow. Just as physical toxins and substances like cholesterol plaque can build up in our arteries and veins, choking off the vital supply of blood, so mental and emotional toxins that collect energetically in and around our chakras inhibit the free flow of energy within us.

> *Think of yourself at all times as an* energy being *as well as a physical one.*
>
> —CAROLINE MYSS

Because each chakra externalizes the energy it receives through a different gland and area of the body, these blockages affect our health, causing us to become fatigued, depressed or even ill. Or maybe we just can't seem to get where we want to go in life. Overstimulating a chakra (by placing continual stress on it), understimulating it (by ignoring it and letting it become weak), or depleting its natural vitality (by unwisely expending its energy) can all create blockages in our body's energetic system.

Since our energy centers are interconnected, what happens in one chakra affects our entire energy system. If any one center is blocked, it can throw the rest of the system off kilter.

Not only that, but the condition of our chakras impacts those we interact with. That's because the energy of our chakras colors and helps create the electromagnetic forcefield, or aura, that surrounds each of us. This energy field interpenetrates and influences the energy field of those around us—for better or for worse. You know how it feels to be around someone who is kind, cheerful and loving in comparison to someone who is depressed or grouchy. Either way, it can be contagious.

Holding On to Energy

It's not just the *quality* of the vibration we send out through our chakras but the *quantity* that can make a difference in our vitality and resilience.

How much energy can we actually hold on to? Those who perpetually get angry have a lot of energy coursing through them, but they can't hold on to it and they don't have a lot of mastery.

It's a simple equation: the more energy we can actually hold on to and master, the more personal power we will have at our disposal. And the more power we have, the more energy we can use to create positive change in our lives and in the lives of those around us. In fact, those who hold an extraordinary energy in their chakras are able to change their corner of the world, and much more than their corner. In this book, you will learn how to recognize when an energy center is blocked and how to clear that block to increase your own vitality and your ability to help others.

Different Ways of Expressing Our Spirituality

Another way to think about the chakras is that each one offers us another way to express our personal spirituality. When you engage the fires of your heart chakra to help someone in need, you have an entirely different experience than when you tap into your creative genius through your crown chakra to teach someone. But they are both ways to get in touch with your spiritual essence and share it.

The direct experience of our spiritual essence is the common thread that unites the mystics of the world's religions. No matter what direction they approach it from, the mystics all seek a direct connection with the divine, whether they call it Christ or Buddha, Tao or Brahman, Allah or Ein Sof or the Great Spirit.

The science of the body's energy centers gives us a practical way of understanding how we tap into the power of the divine—how, as the mystics say, we can become an instrument God can use to reach out into the world. That is the real meaning of empowerment—the power to use the pure energy flowing through us to do good on earth.

Seven Stages of Personal Growth

At each chakra, we have the opportunity to master another dimension of energy and thereby gain another level of awareness, insight and personal power. These rites of passage are stages of personal growth that engage our soul and shape the course of our life. For at each level of awareness, there is a dividing of the real from the unreal, the light from the darkness.

In some traditions, this is known as initiation—the testing of the soul to see how much light she can garner to offset her self-created darkness. These rites of passage are archetypal. Every one of us will face them—no matter who we are, no matter what path we have chosen.

On the pages that follow, we explore the rites of passage corresponding to the chakras. We also share some techniques for smoother sailing through the sometimes narrow straits of life.

How to Use This Book

In today's complex world, the integration of body, mind and soul doesn't necessarily happen by itself. It takes conscious attention and focus, and an awareness of the personal initiations associated with the energy centers.

In this book, you will find keys that can help you with the ABC's of developing your energy centers—activating, balancing and cleansing. Each chapter, devoted to one chakra, reviews the initiations we are called to master. It gives questions for self-reflection, affirmations and spiritual techniques that can help you move through the initiations. These life lessons are not something we face only once. They return to us cyclically, sweeping us up a notch with each turn of the spiral.

We all have areas of strength and areas of weakness. As we walk our individual path of self-transformation, we are meant to use our strengths to overcome our weaknesses. As we become more aware of the archetypal initiations we face, we can identify those areas that need bolstering and concentrate our attention there.

These chapters will help you look for the patterns in your life. If you keep running into the same issue, just dressed up in a new guise or circumstance, take a look at the chakra that corresponds to that issue. See how you can incorporate the keys and techniques in that section to help you work through the issue and move forward. You may want to give some of the affirmations in that chapter or create your own affirmations. You may want to devote a special journal to the meditations and thoughts that come to you as you explore the issues that surface.

As an adjunct to your chakra work, you may also want to experiment with holistic techniques that take an integrated approach to healing. In our final chapter, we review some of the holistic therapies that deal with the physical, emotional and spiritual components of our well-being.

Each energy center is an archetypal matrix, and therefore each one correlates to different attributes, including a different color, part of the body, positive quality, spiritual tradition, musical instrument, and so forth. To help you attune with the chakras, we have listed some of these correlations at the opening of each chapter. Please note that sources vary on which parts of the body each chakra governs.

The seven chakras. . .
are the windows
of the soul.

—DJWAL KUL

In the varied literature on chakras, you will also find differences in the way colors are assigned to the chakras. Some of this information is based on the work of clairvoyants, who can see the vibrations and colors with their "inner" sight. At times the colors denoted by clairvoyants and others may reflect the subdued or even muddied tones that can surround our chakras when they become blocked.

The colors of the chakras given in this book represent how these vibrant vortices of light would appear at spiritual levels if they were working at peak performance. We have found it important when meditating on the chakras to concentrate on the pure, original color patterns.

Finally, there is no magic formula to vitalize your energy centers. The beauty of life is that each of us is spectacularly unique. Like alchemists of the spirit, it is up to us to take the tools in hand and experiment within the laboratory of self. Fortunately for us, personal growth is a creative process and a sacred adventure.

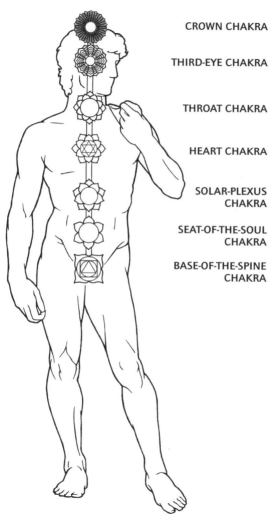

CROWN CHAKRA

THIRD-EYE CHAKRA

THROAT CHAKRA

HEART CHAKRA

SOLAR-PLEXUS
CHAKRA

SEAT-OF-THE-SOUL
CHAKRA

BASE-OF-THE-SPINE
CHAKRA

FIRST ENERGY CENTER:
BASE OF THE SPINE

LOCATION: base of spinal column

COLOR: white

SANSKRIT NAME: Muladhara ("root" and "base," or "foundation")

PETALS: 4

POSITIVE EXPRESSION: purity, hope, joy, self-discipline, integration, perfection, wholeness, nurturing

UNBALANCED EXPRESSION: discouragement, hopelessness, impurity, chaos

PART OF BODY: adrenals

MUSICAL INSTRUMENT: drum, tabla

GEMSTONE: diamond, pearl, zircon, quartz crystal

SPIRITUAL TRADITION: Hinduism

*Through practicality,
self-discipline and joy,
we nurture life to wholeness*

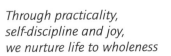

BASE CHAKRA

LIFE LESSON:
Wed the Material
to the Spiritual

*Why separate your spiritual
life and your practical life? To an
integral being, there is no such distinction.*

—LAO TZU

Our ascent begins at the ground level—the level of the energy center known as the base-of-the-spine, or base, chakra. It takes its name from its location at the base of the spine, but it is also the base (foundation) of our inner and outer development. At the base chakra, we access the life-force that enlivens us both physically and spiritually. This energy is the creative power of Spirit anchored in our physical bodies.

The base chakra represents the point where we

connect with the physical world, with nature and with our environment. Balancing the energies of this chakra is therefore fundamental to our practicality and effectiveness in the physical world. When used in harmony, the pure and vibrant energies of the base chakra can endow us with hope, joy, self-discipline and wholeness. Along with the soul chakra, the base also engenders the activity of procreation.

This energy center and its white light are associated with planning, striving for excellence and perfection, and externalizing inner patterns and divine geometry in outer form. The base chakra is also associated with the expression of purity, harmony, perfection, symmetry, order and integration in fields such as music, art, sculpture, architecture, technology and mathematics.

One of the reasons this first energy center is foundational is that its health and vitality affect all the other chakras. How we use the energy that resides at the base chakra will determine whether the potential of our other chakras remains dormant or becomes fully awakened.

Some of us have a greater momentum of mastery in the base chakra than others, but at this level we are all called to learn certain lessons. What are those lessons and initiations? And how can we master the flow of energy through this center?

The ideas we're about to share with you are springboards you can take off on. Your own thoughtful reflection on these concepts, as you carry them with you into daily life, will deepen your understanding of how to accelerate, balance and clear the energies of your first chakra to express more of your inner power.

I value the material world and my body as chalices for Spirit

We cannot evolve spiritually without having a secure physical platform. The two go hand in hand. Sometimes because of our religious upbringing we have the mistaken idea that Spirit is good and matter is bad, or that spiritual things are good but the body is bad. In reality, both the spiritual and the material, in their highest state, are meant to be a reflection of the divine.

Matter comes from the Latin word *mater,* meaning "mother." The physical world *is* the

21

mother because matter is the womb or chalice into which Spirit descends. Matter is the instrument of Spirit. It allows Spirit to express itself. Matter is like the flute and Spirit like the breath. Without our flute—our physical instrument—Spirit cannot play its song through us. And each of us contains a unique song waiting to be heard.

Another misconception we may have is that in order to be spiritual we need to escape from the world around us. But real spirituality isn't leaving the physical world behind; *it's imbuing the physical world with Spirit*. It's being part of the world, but not identifying so much with the material that we forget who we are (spiritual beings) and why we are on earth (to express our spirituality in a practical way as we fulfill our unique reason for being and help others). In other words, being grounded and practical is part and parcel of spirituality.

At the level of the base chakra, we learn to relate to the world in the most meaningful way possible. The initiation at this level asks us to tenderly care for those we are responsible for and not to neglect our duties to others because we are "pursuing spirituality."

In fact, our spirituality demands that we enter

the physical arena. It demands that we integrate the spiritual and the material. Ramana Maharshi, one of the great spiritual teachers of modern India, once chided a student who wanted to give up his job and family to serve God. He said, "Renunciation doesn't mean giving away your money or abandoning your home. . . . No: a true renunciate actually merges in the world and expands his love to embrace the whole world."[1]

It's like Aesop's fable of the astronomer who would wander around the town each night studying the skies. One night while he was staring up at the heavens, he fell into a deep well. The neighbor who finally heard his cries said, "Why probe the skies when you can't even see what's here on the earth?"

Another lesson we learn at the level of the base chakra is to have a positive view of our body and to build a working relationship with our body. When we have a healthy regard for the physical world and for our own physical bodies, we become a much better partner with Spirit. If we are to fulfill our unique mission in life, we need to be strong at the mental, emotional, spiritual *and* physical levels.

God wants us to take care of our body—to

listen to what our body is telling us and to understand what it needs. Each of us has different needs.
Your best friend may be able to eat a wonderfully
rich dessert after lunch, but the same dessert might
floor you for the rest of the day. She may be able

*Strengthen your
body before you
strengthen your soul.*

—RABBI NACHMAN
OF BRATSLAV

to stay up half the night
but you just can't do it.

Caring for yourself
by cultivating a positive
attitude about your body,
taking time to get the
nourishment, exercise and
rest you need, and getting

good advice from health-care professionals when
needed can help you get fit spiritually.

At energetic levels, the reason it's important to
pay attention to the physical is that the condition
of our body determines in part how much energy
we are able to hold on to. If you could plug a 120-
volt desk lamp into a 240-volt outlet, the light
bulb would burn out. Likewise, God won't let a
240-volt flash of light pour through you if the chalice of your body is only able to receive a 120-volt
charge of light.

Our care for the physical includes not only

our body but our physical base. Our home and our work environment are extensions and expressions of our soul—the crucibles in which we forge our life's work. "Care for our actual houses," says psychotherapist and author Thomas Moore, "is also care of the soul. No matter how little money we have, we can be mindful of the importance of beauty in our homes."[2] The more uplifted we are by our environment, the more creative and fulfilled we will be.

Is my spirituality practical?

Can I perform effectively at the physical level of existence? Or do I tend to ignore physical demands and keep my head in the clouds— or in the sand?

When my body shows signs that it is out of balance, do I take the necessary action to get back into balance?

How can I enhance my home and work space to encourage and inspire my creativity?

I strive to be nonattached to my belongings

Most of the lessons associated with our seven energy centers have to do with balance. While we value the material world as a way to concretely express our spirituality, overattachment to the physical can tempt us into materialism. The challenge can be subtler than we realize. Even the poorest person can become a materialist if he is overly concerned about his possessions (or lack of them) and resents those who have more than he does. Lao Tzu taught, "To know when you have enough is to be rich." And that "enough" is different for each of us.

A famous rabbi in Poland revealed this truth to a tourist, who was surprised to see that the rabbi lived in only one room. It contained many books but just a bench and a table. "Where is your furniture?" the visitor asked.

"Where is yours?" the rabbi retorted.

The tourist shrugged his shoulders and explained that he, of course, didn't have any furniture with him because he was just visiting.

"Well," replied the rabbi, "I am too."

The rabbi knew that we are all just visitors on planet earth. This isn't our final destination, so why should we be attached to its accoutrements?

At the other end of the spectrum, some feel that spirituality and prosperity don't mix. It all depends on our definition of prosperity and our attitude toward our belongings. Do we see our belongings and our resources as extensions, as instruments, of our spirituality?

The twentieth-century Indian spiritual leader Sri Aurobindo saw money as a resource that should be used to reconnect us with our Divine Source. He taught that it is not necessary to completely renounce all money, just as it is unhealthy to be attached to it.

"All wealth belongs to the Divine and those who hold it are trustees, not possessors," he said. "It is with them today; tomorrow it may be elsewhere. . . . In your personal use of money, look on all you have or get or bring as the [Divine] Mother's. . . . Always consider that it is her possessions and not your own that you are handling. . . . Do not look up to men because of their riches or allow yourself to be impressed by the show, the power, or the influence."[3]

What do I need to sustain the physical platform of my life and support my family's needs?

 Do I deny myself the things I need? Or do I indulge in things I don't need?

 When does my focus on the material become an obstruction to my spiritual goals?

 I look beyond outer appearances to the inner essence

As we master the energies of the base chakra, we move from attachment to the outer form to an appreciation of the inner essence. Another name for attachment to the outer is idolatry. Idolatry is placing one's trust in the vessel that houses the Spirit instead of placing one's trust in the spiritual flame that abides in the vessel. When we meet someone, do we take a reading based on what they look like and what they are wearing—or do we take a moment to tune into the inner qualities they are expressing?

Barry and Joyce Vissell offer a poignant example

of this in their book *The Shared Heart*:

"Moses Mendelssohn, the grandfather of the well-known German composer, was far from being a handsome man. Along with a rather short stature, he also possessed a grotesque humpback.

"Once, he visited a Hamburg merchant [who had] a lovely daughter named Frumtje. Moses fell hopelessly in love with this young woman. But alas, Frumtje was repulsed by his misshapen appearance.

"Finally, the time came for farewells. Moses gathered his courage and climbed the stairs to her room. She was a vision of heavenly beauty, but caused him deep sadness by her refusal to even look up at him. After several attempts at conversation, Moses shyly questioned, 'Do you believe marriages are made in heaven?'

"'Yes,' she answered, still looking at the floor. 'And do you?'

"'Yes, I do,' he replied. 'You see, in heaven at the birth of each boy, the Lord announces, "This boy will marry that particular girl." And when I was born, my future bride was pointed out to me, and then the Lord added, "But your wife will be humpbacked."

"'Right then and there I called out, "Oh Lord,

a humpbacked woman would be a tragedy. Please, Lord, give me the hump and let her be beautiful."

"Then Frumtje looked up into his eyes, and was stirred by some deep memory. She reached out and gave Mendelssohn her hand, and later became his devoted wife."[4] At that moment, the young girl was able to see beyond outer appearances to the inner essence.

Idolatry and its sidekicks—overdependence and codependence—are especially challenging in relationships. In a healthy relationship, each partner can stand on a firm foundation of his own. It has to be that way so the partners can take turns bolstering each other. If one of them hasn't developed his own strong roots, the relationship isn't really a partnership at all.

Kahlil Gibran eloquently captured this truth when he wrote of marriage: "Let there be spaces in your togetherness. . . . Sing and dance together and be joyous, but let each one of you be alone, even as the strings of a lute are alone though they quiver with the same music. . . . Stand together yet not too near together: for the pillars of the temple stand apart, and the oak tree and the cypress grow not in each other's shadow."[5]

We are called to love, respect and honor the spirit that expresses itself through others. But if we create an idol out of our partner, then we short-change our own spiritual path, which requires us to forge our special one-on-one relationship with God. That is one relationship that no one can replace and no one can fill. If you try to put someone else in place of God, at some level you will always be disappointed. There is a certain place in your being where only you and God can go.

When we idolize anything—whether it's a person or outer accoutrements—to the exclusion of the spiritual side of life, God may give us a wake-up call. That person or that thing may be taken away from us for a season so that we can focus our energies on what is most important to our spiritual growth right now. Once we have reestablished our balance, we are often able to reincorporate what was taken away into our life again.

How can I remind myself to look beyond outer trappings to the inner essence?

Have I allowed someone or something to take the place of my relationship with God?

*I honor the sacred in nature
and apply its lessons to my life*

Another way we enhance our connection with Spirit at the level of the base chakra is to strengthen our connection with Mother Nature. Our Native American brethren have much to teach us in this regard. Chief Luther Standing Bear said the Native Americans sat or reclined on the ground with a feeling of being close to "a mothering power." He said, "The old Indian still sits upon the earth instead of propping himself up and away from its life-giving forces" because he is "able to think more deeply and to feel more keenly."

Working with the earth, with plants and with animals increases our sensitivity to life. We learn to tune into what that plant needs in order to flourish. Does it have enough sunlight and the right amount of water? Does its soil have the proper nutrients? We can apply the same sensitivity to the way we care for others. People also need care and attention. They too need optimum conditions in order to flourish.

Many of us had special experiences with nature when we were growing up. As adults we sometimes lose that sense of oneness with Mother Nature or forget that she has anything more to teach us. Take Susanna.* At forty-one, things just didn't seem to be working out the way she expected in her marriage or in her career. She blamed herself. She had convinced herself that there must be something wrong with her at a very fundamental level.

Nearness to nature... keeps the spirit sensitive to impressions not commonly felt, and in touch with the unseen powers.

—OHIYESA
(DR. CHARLES A. EASTMAN)

After work one evening she took a walk nearby her home, wondering why she didn't do it more often. It was summer's end and the air was crisp and fresh. The treetops sang their special song as they moved in the wind. The brook alongside the path playfully embraced the rocks. Everything was magical—from the tiniest caterpillar to the sprawling oak trees.

How beautiful is everything God makes! she thought. Then, with a sudden, gentle burst of illumination, that truth echoed within her: *God made*

---

*The names in the stories throughout this book have been changed.

33

me. Therefore I must be beautiful in my own special way. The magic is inside of me too.

At that moment, she gained a new perspective of herself. She had to keep reinforcing that vision, but nature had brought her an invaluable lesson that helped her grow in the months and years to come.

 Do I honor and respect nature and the environment?

 Do I allow myself time to connect with nature?

 Have my experiences with nature taught me any gentle or thunderous lessons that I need to remind myself of today?

 I honor, respect and nurture the feminine in myself and others

The energy of the base chakra is also referred to as the "Mother light." In a spiritually symbolic sense, the physical universe, which is associated with the base chakra, represents the feminine (or Mother)

34

principle of God. The spiritual universe represents the masculine (or Father) principle.

Most of us grew up with only a partial understanding of God. We learned a lot about the masculine side of the divine world—God the Father, God the Son—the side that protects and disciplines, sets standards and enforces limits. But as the inner traditions of the world's religions show us, there is another side of the divine: the feminine side, or God the Mother. This side nurtures, teaches and supports. She is the sacred energy that comforts and heals. The base chakra corresponds to this feminine aspect of life.

The concept of a divine Mother embraces and yet transcends all religions. In Jewish tradition, the feminine aspect of God is called Shekhinah, literally "Divine Presence." In Hinduism she appears as Shakti, in Buddhism as Prajnaparamita, and in Egyptian tradition as Isis. In some texts of the Old Testament and Apocrypha, the feminine aspect of the divine is called Wisdom, just as the Christian gnostics called her Sophia or Pistis Sophia (meaning "Faith-Wisdom").

These personifications of the feminine are not, at their core, goddesses to be worshiped. They are embodiments of the feminine attributes of God who teach us by example how we can realize our *own* feminine potential. We all have a feminine side. It is sensitive, intuitive, creative. It is the side of us that develops and maintains relationships. It is nourishing, patient and joyful. The healthy feminine side is not distant or abandoning. Neither is it possessive or smothering.

When we maintain a vital and balanced flow of energy through the base chakra, we are able to express the caring qualities of the divine feminine. We too become sensitive to the needs of others.

Again taking an analogy from nature, a plant that needs water doesn't speak to us and tell us it's thirsty. Its soil becomes parched and its leaves droop and finally drop off. In the same way, people who need our care often don't tell us what their problems are. We have to look for the signs and figure out what they really mean. A sullen face doesn't always mean that someone dislikes us. It may mean they need us to notice that something's wrong. When we "mother" life, we look behind outer appearances to what's really happening on the inside.

I had a profound realization of this years ago

when I was in Rome standing before the *Pietà*. As I meditated upon the sublime form of Mary holding her crucified son, I realized that the "mother" within each of us is called to succor those who are helpless, those who need our unconditional love and support. We are all in this circumstance at one time or another, and we are all called to fill the role of mother at one time or another.

At the level of the base chakra, we are also compelled to examine our relationship with women, with the feminine aspect of ourselves and with our soul. Do we honor and respect women? Even though we have to be on the front lines in the business world, do we express our feminine side—whether we are a man or woman—and appreciate others who do? Do we take time to nurture ourselves?

If as a child you were separated from your mother or you did not bond to her, you may find it hard to nurture yourself and come to grips with your real soul needs. Just remember: the proper food for the soul is as important as the proper nourishment for the body.

What makes you happy? What soothes you when you are troubled? Is it music? poetry? a good novel? Is it using your hands to make pottery or sew? Is it meditating? Is it a jog or a workout at the gym? What is it that creates magical moments for you?

It can be as simple as buying fresh flowers to put on your desk once a week, or periodically framing a new picture to hang on your wall. Maybe it's taking time to play with a child or to hike along a forest path.

 What can I do this week to express my feminine side—the intuitive, sensitive, nurturing side of my nature?

 What soul food am I missing, and how can I set aside adequate time and space to meet my soul's needs?

 I conserve my energy

Those who conserve the energy they receive from their Source are the most creative, joyous and effective people in all fields of endeavor—because they are overflowing with that spiritual energy and they want to share it with others.

What does it mean to "conserve" energy? Every day we receive from our Source an allotment of spiritual energy. This is the energy that empowers us to think, feel, speak and act. As I said earlier, we have free will to decide what to do with that energy. We can—through loving deeds and our spiritual practices—raise that sacred fire to endow all our interactions with that vitality of spirit.

On the other hand, we can dissipate that energy in any one of our chakras through a number of unbalanced activities that don't add value to our spiritual path. These could include anything from outbursts of anger to excessive chattering, egoism, criticism, gossip, resentment, nonforgiveness, perverted or excessive sexual activity, jealousy, obsession with material objects, feeling sorry for ourselves, revolving the past, constantly worrying about the future, and so on.

The bottom line is this: We waste God's precious energy by diverting it into activities that are not helping us grow spiritually—activities that tie up our energy rather than letting it flow. The best measuring rod is to ask yourself: *Is what I'm about to do helping me realize more of my spiritual nature? Is it helping me integrate my spirituality into everyday life? Is it allowing me to help others in a meaningful way?*

When we conserve the energy (the Kundalini) that resides at the base-of-the-spine chakra, it naturally rises to nourish our other centers, activating new levels of spiritual awareness within us. If we dissipate or block it from rising, two things can happen. First, we reduce the amount of energy available to rise through the other chakras, and thus the latent power of those chakras remains untapped.

If you do not care about your vitality and waste it arbitrarily, that is like putting water into a leaking cup.

—ANCESTOR LÜ

Second, if our focus remains merely on the physical and goes no higher, energy can build up at the level of the base chakra. When too much energy collects at the base, it demands an outlet. In some individuals this has resulted in rampages of anger, physical abuse or the misuse of sexual energy.

Both the base chakra and the seat-of-the-soul chakra are associated with sexuality. We can create an imbalance in our base chakra if we have an inordinate focus on sexual activity or an inordinate fear of sexuality. Many spiritual traditions teach that sexual activity in balance and in the right context is healthy. Sex is a sacred energy exchange *(s-e-x)*. Sacred sexuality can be an intimate experience with God and with the divine energy residing within us and within our partner. For that very reason, it is important to treat our relationships as sacred and be careful about getting into a relationship just to mark time.

When we are in any relationship, we are investing our precious energy in it, and we are allowing another to be in a position of polarity with us for the exchange of energy. We want to be sure we're investing that energy wisely. This goes for all kinds of relationships and partnerships. Sometimes people want to hang on to a friendship or a partnership or a relationship that isn't healthy "until something better comes along." Yet they haven't created the vacuum or amplified the magnet of light within to attract the partner who is right for them. When we attend to our own spiritual wholeness, we automatically attract the right partners.

It comes down to the fact that the more we conserve our life-force, the more energy we have available for physical, emotional and spiritual vitality. If we don't conserve that energy, we may not have the inner resources to cope with the details of life, much less attend to the deeper issues of our spiritual growth.

 Am I diverting my energy into activities or relationships that are not helping me grow?

 Are there ways I can better conserve my energy?

Working with the Base Chakra

A word of caution about working with the base chakra. As we work with each of the life lessons of the base chakra and use our energy wisely, the energy of our base chakra will naturally and gradually rise. As it does, we will not necessarily feel it in a physical sense because it is taking place at inner levels of our being.

There are several techniques that claim to accelerate the raising of the Kundalini. However, unless the base chakra is first balanced and cleared, these practices can be dangerous. For as the energy rises, it can activate the negatives that we are carrying around with us. For this reason, I have found it best to meditate on the upper chakras, from the heart to the crown. When we intensify the light of our upper chakras, they become magnets of light that naturally and safely draw up the energy from the base chakra.

An effective way to purify and accelerate all our chakras is to access the high-frequency spiritual energy known as the violet flame through prayer and meditation (see pages 89–95). The meditation and affirmation on the following pages can also help balance and clear the base chakra.

SPIRITUAL TECHNIQUES

Mantra for the Resurrection of the Inner Light

Visualization:

As you say the following affirmation, see and feel the light within you as a mother-of-pearl softness bathing your body in a gentle, suffusing glow. See the light surround every cell and atom of your body, becoming whiter and whiter. As the cells and atoms accelerate, they begin to spin—releasing the white light to clear and energize your body, mind and emotions.

As you recite this affirmation, stand with your arms raised over your head. Imagine that you are directing the energy that is rising up the network of your chakras back to God.

*I AM the resurrection and the life
of every cell and atom of my being
now made manifest!*

Note: You can say this affirmation whenever you feel that the energy flow in some area of your life is blocked, replacing the words "every cell and atom of my being" with the specific area of your life you want to rejuvenate.

SECOND ENERGY CENTER:
SEAT OF THE SOUL

LOCATION: midway between the navel and base of the spine

COLOR: violet

SANSKRIT NAME: Svadhishthana ("sweetness" or "abode of the self")

PETALS: 6

POSITIVE EXPRESSION: freedom, mercy, forgiveness, justice, transcendence, alchemy, transmutation, diplomacy, intuition, prophecy, revelation

UNBALANCED EXPRESSION: lack of forgiveness, justice or mercy; intolerance, lack of tact, disregard for others, cruelty

PART OF BODY: organs and systems of elimination and reproduction

MUSICAL INSTRUMENT: woodwinds

GEMSTONE: amethyst, diamond, aquamarine

SPIRITUAL TRADITION: Taoism

By reclaiming our soul's original pattern, we are free to realize our full creative potential

SOUL CHAKRA

LIFE LESSON:
To Thine Own
Self Be True

*Man's main task in
life is to give birth to himself.*

—ERICH FROMM

Through the second energy center, the seat-of-the-soul chakra, we experience freedom—the freedom to become all that we are meant to be. The ancients saw the seat of the soul as a real power point. In the martial arts, it is our point of equilibrium and the central focus of ch'i, the inner energy essential to the maintenance of life.

This chakra is also the point where we make contact with our soul and receive her impressions and guidance. Our soul is wise and can give us much inner direction. We all have soul powers. When you have a gut feeling about someone, you are receiving an instantaneous soul impression. Sometimes your soul will give you a warning, "It's not safe to go here or to do this right now..." It's part of your internal guidance system.

More often than not, these impressions and intuitions are accurate. The more our soul is in touch with her true, spiritual nature, the more sensitive and accurate these readings will be. The more our soul is attached to the human ego, the unreal self, the less clear these readings will be. The initiations of the seat-of-the-soul chakra deal with expressing our soul's true voice and her creative impulses. At the level of the seat of the soul, we also deal with archetypes, patterns and personality.

I invest my energy in ways that are congruent with my soul's original inheritance and pattern

The powers of procreation in man and woman are anchored through the soul chakra. The seed and the egg pass on physical and karmic patterns through the genes and chromosomes. They also pass on the spiritual matrix of our identity—our spiritual inheritance.

The soul retains an ancient memory, even if it's dim, of her divine origin, her divine pattern and the part she is to play in God's scheme. Although our soul is meant to be a clear reflecting pool for that original pattern, sometimes the waters get muddied. On her journey through the ages, our soul has at times taken on patterns that are not in alignment with her divine pattern.

Too many of us have had the experience of trying to work out our life's mission while someone else, well-meaning or not, has tried to impose on us *their* version of our life plan. Your opportunity at the level of the soul chakra is to recapture the original matrix of your soul-identity—to be true to yourself. Your challenge is to free your soul to recognize and then fully claim your spiritual inheritance and pattern. As seventeenth-century Kabbalist Moses Zacuto wrote, "Search and discover the root of your soul, so that you can fulfill it and restore it to its source, its essence. The more you fulfill yourself, the closer you approach your authentic self."[1]

Self-knowledge—knowledge of our real self

and our real path in life—is the starting point of our personal power and our soul liberation. The soul that is truly free is the soul that can express her native reality.

If we didn't have role models or caregivers who encouraged us to tune into and cultivate our unique soul-identity, we may have never even glimpsed the real plan for our soul. If we had parents or other strong authority figures who imposed their will on us, we may find that part of us is chasing after someone else's dreams.

The main condition for progress is honesty with oneself.

—HELENA ROERICH

In order to balance our energies at the level of the seat of the soul, we need to determine if we are letting our energy flow into byways that someone else has carved for us. We will never be totally happy, at peace or fulfilled if we don't reclaim that energy and redirect it back into the mainstream of our life.

What is the unique mission I am called to fulfill in this life?

Am I allowing my energies to travel in byways that are not a part of my soul pattern and my life's purpose?

I regularly and honestly appraise how much of my identity is invested in my human ego or in my real self

When we are on a spiritual path, we discover that the greatest challenges come not from without but from within. As the cartoon character Pogo once said, "We have met the enemy—and they is us!"

The road to self-mastery is a continual process of self-examination. We must have the courage to explore how much of our identity is invested in our true, divine nature and how much is invested in our lower nature, our human ego. Kabbalists called this darker side of our nature "the evil urge." Saint Paul referred to it as "the carnal mind." In esoteric tradition it is known as the dweller-on-the-threshold.

We all have a Mr. Hyde who comes unexpectedly popping out when we least expect it. Mahatma Gandhi once quipped: "I have only three enemies.

My favorite enemy, the one most easily influenced for the better, is the British Empire. My second enemy, the Indian people, is far more difficult. But my most formidable opponent is a man named Mohandas K. Gandhi. With him I seem to have very little influence."

The long and short of it is that the human ego is the impostor of our real self. At the level of the seat of the soul, we begin to recognize which aspects of our personality are part of our real nature and which are not. This is not necessarily a comfortable place to be, but it is the only *real* place to be.

In the gnostic Gospel of Thomas, Jesus says that the pain of facing this truth will be troubling, but it is a necessary first step in overcoming and self-mastery. It is the catalyst that will impel us to unleash all of our hidden potential. Jesus says, "Let him who seeks continue seeking until he finds. When he finds, he will become troubled. When he becomes troubled, he will be astonished, and he will rule over the all."[2]

The initiation of the soul chakra gives us the opportunity to free ourselves from those aspects of our personality that are not part of our true identity —our "mask," as Mark Prophet often called it.[3]

Sometimes we develop this persona because we think it is what other people expect from us, even though it isn't the real us.

If we want the full beauty of our real self to unfold, we need to peel away the layers of the mask surrounding it. "Man knows so many things; he does not know himself," observed fourteenth-century mystic Meister Eckhart. "Why, thirty or forty skins or hides, just like an ox's or a bear's so thick and hard, cover the soul. Go into your own ground and learn to know yourself there."

What can we do if we have identified patterns in our world that we no longer want to claim as our own? First we have to know that through the pure energy of the seat-of-the-soul chakra, we are not prisoners of our past. We can create new energy patterns.

We also have to realize that our habit patterns, which we have created over many years or embodiments, can't be uncreated in a day. They won't disappear until we get to the core of why our soul developed those thick skins in the first place. There were plenty of good reasons. The soul is sensitive and impressionable, and although we don't consciously remember all the experiences we've had in all of our embodiments, our soul does. This includes unpleasant experiences where our soul was wounded. When we go through physical or emotional trauma, we don't just feel it in our body

or in our emotions; we feel it in our soul as well.

If you will not know yourselves, you dwell in poverty.

—JESUS IN THE GOSPEL OF THOMAS

To protect herself and alleviate her pain, the wounded soul develops certain behaviors, defense mechanisms, that can adversely affect subsequent relationships in her life, inhibit the development of her true self, and create a blockage in the body's energy system.

We all have some energy tied up in patterns that are not healthy for us. When we heal the wounded part of our soul, we can liberate this energy to use in the here and now.

Many times the healing process requires serious attention to the issues of our psychology (literally, the study of the psyche, or soul) and we can gain strides by working with a trained therapist who understands the spiritual path. Patterns become entrenched, and creating new ones takes skilled coaching as well as profound inner work.

As Jungian analyst Edward Edinger wrote: "Psychological development in all its phases is a redemptive process. The goal is to redeem by conscious realization the hidden Self, hidden in unconscious identification with the ego."[4] We can accelerate this soul work by applying spiritual tools, such as prayers, mantras, meditations and visualizations. Both the psychological and spiritual work are often necessary for deep soul healing.

 What parts of my personality do I feel reflect the real me?

 What habit patterns have I developed that do not support my spiritual growth?

I am able to tap into and freely express my creative impulses

Moment by moment we create. Whatever we answer to the question "What have I done with my energy today?" is our day's creation. Our thoughts, words, actions and feelings are our creations. When we are on a spiritual path we realize the importance of these creations and we take accountability for the impact our thoughts, words and deeds have on others.

Again, we have just so much energy allotted to us each day. Where do we invest it? What do we create with it? And do we feel blocked in our ability to create because of feelings of guilt, frustration or inadequacy?

Health practitioners have shown that ailments in the area of the seat of the soul—corresponding to the organs of reproduction and elimination—are sometimes related to an unresolved issue with creativity. When we feel "stuck" and cannot express our innate creativity, then our emotions and body reflect this tension.

I know of several cases where women who felt boxed in were plagued with chronic health problems in the breast and uterus until they came to grips with this issue. Janice and Ellen, for example, were always filled with new ideas, but their work environment would not allow them to give their gifts. As a result, both were apt to revolve their situations and complain heavily, feeling powerless to break out of their boxes. Both began to develop health problems.

Eventually, Janice was forced to make a job change—a hidden blessing that opened the door for her to follow her heart and take on responsibilities that allowed her to blossom. Ellen, in her fifties, took the bold step of going back to school to pursue her real passion. Both are thriving, and their emotions and health show it.

When Janice and Ellen finally stopped and listened to their soul intuition, a new world opened up for them. That's what can happen when we commune with our soul through our soul chakra. When we aren't able to tune into the voice of our soul, it's

I can find nothing with which to compare the great beauty of a soul and its great capacity.

—TERESA OF AVILA

sometimes because our overactive or domineering intellect has suppressed our soul senses.

Our intellect is a wonderful vessel for our Higher Self to work through, but the reasoning, educated mind alone will not create that important connection to our soul. In fact, it can short-circuit it. "There is a mode of knowing that is above intelligence," said the fifth-century Neoplatonic philosopher Proclus. "Let the intelligent soul transcend intelligence. . . . This, my friend, is the divine working of the soul."

The intellect cannot take the place of our soul. That is why the education of the heart and soul is just as important as the education of our mind. To create a safe harbor for the soul, we sometimes have to turn off the intellect and consciously enter into the heart and soul to get in touch with our inner creative self.

🏵 *Am I able to express my creativity, or do I feel stifled in any way? What steps can I take to get unstuck?*

🏵 *Do my home and my work environment encourage me to be creative?*
If not, what changes can I make?

🏵 *What helps me to set aside my intellect and logical mind for a moment and tap into my inner creative self through my soul senses? How can I incorporate more of that into my daily life?*

I free myself from old patterns by forgiving myself and others

An essential part of the process of freeing ourselves from old patterns is encapsulated in a single word: *forgiveness*. If we do not forgive the wrongs and injustices practiced against us, we allow ourselves to be tied, through the law of karma, to the one who has wronged us.

The old vendettas that individuals, families and even nations hold against one another go on for centuries for this very reason. Their warring never ends because their hatred forms a strong rope between themselves and their enemies— a rope that grows thicker and thicker the more they hate. When those involved reincarnate, they carry the same entrenched energy patterns with them, and the vendettas live on and on.

Resentment is a vicious circle. It drains us of our energy because part of us is always focused on that unresolved situation. As Emerson put it, when this is the case "we are not free to use today, or to promise tomorrow, because we are already mortgaged to yesterday." When we forgive, we free up 100 percent of our energy for constructive endeavor.

There may be times when we feel we cannot forgive someone. We believe the crime he or she has committed against us or a loved one has just been too great. God has taught me that in a situation like this we can embrace the soul and then ask God and his angels to bind the unreal self, the dark side, of the person that caused him to commit the crime.

No matter how bad a person's deeds are, if we forgive the soul—that part of his being that still has the potential for good—we can avoid a karmic entanglement. When we hold on to these unpleasant experiences, our energy gets knotted up and we create an energy blockage.

It's never really a personal issue, no matter how personal it seems. The situation is often a testing ground—an opportunity to see if we've developed forgiveness and compassion. Mother Teresa once said, "People are often unreasonable, illogical, and self-centered; forgive them anyway. If you are kind, people may accuse you of selfish, ulterior motives; be kind anyway.... If you are honest and frank, people may cheat you; be honest and frank anyway.... You see, in the final analysis, it is between you and God; it was never between you and them anyway."

Often the hardest part of letting go is forgiving *ourselves*—realizing that no matter what mistakes we have made, at the time we made them we were doing the best we could. We don't have to deny the mistake, but we do have to get over it. We have to tell ourselves, "The mistake was no good, but I'm still a good person," and then learn from the experience. Making mistakes is the way we learn. As Thomas Edison said, "I have not failed. I've just found 10,000 ways that won't work."

Sometimes we don't even realize that not forgiving ourselves is what's holding us back. Victoria came to this soul awareness on her road to healing. In her early thirties, she found out that she had breast cancer. "After the initial shock," she says, "it took me a while to realize that this was a warning—not only from my body, but from my soul. I had to come to grips with the fact that I was wearing myself out (the message from my body) and I wasn't having much fun in the process (the message from my soul).

"After my surgery, I changed my diet and adjusted my schedule. Physically, I was on the road to recovery. But emotionally, I was still in a crisis.

I had hit a stone wall and I didn't know how to get around it.

"One day I just broke down. And out of the midst of my tears, I could hear my anguished soul giving me the key: I had been beating up on myself ever since I had found out the news. All this time, I had believed that I was a 'bad' person because I had gotten sick. I had never forgiven myself for the cancer—because I didn't think I was worthy of forgiveness. That was the wall.

"Before I could move forward, I had to get to the point where I valued myself enough to accept that I may not have done anything 'wrong,' and even if I had, I was worthy of forgiveness.

"It wasn't easy wending my way through this labyrinth of misconceptions I had somehow taken in. But as I moved through the process, changes took place. I started to blossom. I started having more fun. And the real me came out of hiding."

Gautama Buddha once said, "You can look the whole world over and never find anyone more deserving of love than yourself." If we want to make lasting changes in our lives, we have to love our soul—and we have to patiently nurture it through the healing process.

*Is there someone I need to forgive—
for my own liberation and their liberation?*

 *Is there something I've never forgiven
myself for that is holding me back? Is there
a fundamental misconception about myself
that is preventing me from extending mercy
to my own soul?*

SPIRITUAL TECHNIQUES

Affirmation for Forgiveness

The apostle Paul counseled us, "Let not the sun go down upon your wrath." If we are able to let go of all sense of injustice and anger at the end of each day (even guilt about our own shortcomings), we will be on the road to better health, greater peace and true happiness.

Visualization:

In those moments just before you fall asleep, close your eyes and let the events of the day pass before you like a movie. Call to mind the people who need your love and forgiveness. Ask God to forgive them and to forgive you.

Then see violet light, which is the native light of the soul chakra, passing through these scenes. See this violet light turn into intense flames of violet. Watch these flames neutralize the negative impact of the day's events.

As you give the following affirmation, focus your attention on your heart. Send love and forgiveness to all those you have wronged and all who have wronged you, releasing the situations into God's hands. You can repeat this affirmation as many times as you feel the need to.

Forgiveness

I AM forgiveness acting here,
Casting out all doubt and fear,
Setting men forever free
With wings of cosmic victory.

I AM calling in full power
For forgiveness every hour;
To all life in every place
I flood forth forgiving grace.

THIRD ENERGY CENTER:
SOLAR PLEXUS

LOCATION: at the navel

COLOR: purple and gold with ruby flecks

SANSKRIT NAME: Manipura
  ("city of jewels" or "filled with jewels")

PETALS: 10

POSITIVE EXPRESSION: peace, brotherhood, selfless service, right desire, balance, harmlessness

UNBALANCED EXPRESSION: anger, agitation, fanaticism, aggression, egoism, overindulgence, fear, anxiety, passivity

PART OF BODY: digestive system, liver, pancreas

MUSICAL INSTRUMENT: organ

GEMSTONE: topaz, ruby, alexandrite, diamond with pearl

SPIRITUAL TRADITION: Islam

By mastering emotion and desire, we cultivate inner peace, brotherhood and selfless service

SOLAR-PLEXUS CHAKRA

LIFE LESSON:
Walk the Middle
Way of Balance

The impulse "I want" and
the impulse "I'll have"—lose them!
That is where most people get stuck.
—THE SUTTA-NIPATA

The next step in our voyage of self-discovery is to rise from the seat-of-the-soul chakra to the level of the solar plexus. Here the soul learns to cultivate inner peace and brotherhood. She does this by mastering her emotions and desires while dealing with the tests and trials of her karma.

The solar plexus, from which this chakra takes its name, is the large network of nerves located behind the stomach. Most of us have felt butterflies in our belly or a wallop of energy from someone who was upset with us, as if we were being punched in the stomach. We were processing those emotions through the energy center at the solar plexus.

Feelings like anger, agitation or fear as well as spiritual feelings of peace or devotion are filtered through this center. Our solar-plexus and throat centers are closely linked, for we often express our feelings through our speech. So powerful are our emotions that the solar-plexus chakra can multiply—for blessing or bane—what is taking place through our other chakras.

 I engage the power of my emotions as an instrument of peace

When Jesus said, "out of his belly shall flow rivers of living water," he was talking about those who would become instruments of peace as they mastered the powerful currents flowing through the solar-plexus chakra.

Mastering the emotions does not mean that we have no emotion. Emotion *(e-motion)* is simply *energy in motion.* We can use our energy in motion to reflect and amplify the feelings of our soul or we can use it to subject the soul. We can use our energy in motion to emanate peace or to amplify agitation—to inspire or to provoke.

By staying calm when everything around us is in chaos, by tapping into the powerful reservoir of peace that can be garnered in the solar plexus, we can summon a tremendous sea of energy to stabilize a situation, whether it is in our home or in a crowd. Jack Kornfield tells a story about the Cambodian monk Maha Gosananda that shows the power we can wield through a peaceful solar-plexus chakra.

The hero is the man who is immovably centered.

—RALPH WALDO EMERSON

Maha Gosananda was visiting thousands of Cambodian refugees who had fled the ravages of Pol Pot. The monk invited them to a Buddhist ceremony, and over ten thousand refugees gathered for the event. Maha Gosananda was silent for some time. Before him were people who had been deeply wounded, whose family members had been killed, whose homes and temples had been destroyed.

69

He began to chant a verse from the Dhammapada: "Hatred never ceases by hatred but by love alone is healed. This is an ancient and eternal law." Soon the entire group of refugees, moved by this timeless truth, joined him in chanting this refrain.

Maha Gosananda could have taken advantage of their frustration and anger. Instead, he chose to help them tap into the reservoir of peace and love that Pol Pot could never take from them.

"If you're quiet and tranquil," taught Lao Tzu, "you can become the ruler of the world." Likewise, the author of Proverbs advised, "He that is slow to anger is better than the mighty; and he that ruleth his spirit than he that taketh a city."

The test of the emotions comes in big and little ways, tempting us to indulge the emotions or lose control of them. Sometimes these tests are the way our karma[1] knocks upon our door as our past actions return to us for resolution in the form of current circumstances. Sometimes the initiation is a training ground. In school we take our lessons to master certain subjects. It's no different in real life, except it's a lot less theoretical and a lot more practical.

God wants us to master our lessons in energy flow, and he needs to make sure we've got it right.

For God will not give us more energy than we can hold in the chalice of our chakras and put to good use. Why do we want to have a reserve of energy? So that when the necessity arises we can send out to others, through our chakras and our aura, the healing light of joy, freedom, peace, love, power, vision and wisdom.

It's like taking out a loan. If we prove that we can use God's energy wisely for the good of others, he knows that his investment is safe. If we misuse that energy—by becoming angry or agitated, for instance—eventually our supply will be cut off because we haven't shown that we can use it responsibly.

So when you are confronted with the trials of life that seem to be trying to unseat you, it's because you're doing something *right,* not something wrong. When we're committed to a course of spiritual growth, we can expect that we'll be tested. As Booker T. Washington once said, "Success is not measured by the position one has reached in life, rather by the obstacles overcome while trying to succeed."

That's what that quizzical verse we learned in Sunday school was all about: "Count it all joy when ye fall into divers temptations; knowing this, that the trying of your faith worketh patience. But let patience have her perfect work, that ye may be perfect and entire."[2] "Difficulties are the very road to immortality," said Lao Tzu, advising us to meet them "calmly and openly, however they unfold."[3]

In the case of the solar plexus, our exams give us the opportunity to express our self-control. They give us the opportunity to show that our love for God—and our gratitude for the precious energy of life he showers upon us daily—is greater than our need to let off steam, even if someone else is sending anger, aggression, anxiety or agitation our way.

Self-conquest is, indeed, far greater than the conquest of all other folk.

—THE DHAMMAPADA

Tibetan Buddhism teaches that anger is one of the "poisons" that are deadly to our spiritual growth. Through anger we can very quickly lose any ground we have gained. Like a baby who cries until he is literally exhausted, tirades of anger or other forms of emotional abuse can exhaust our energy supply—and cause turmoil within the energy centers of others.

Anger, of course, is a symptom of a deeper

72

malaise, telling us to dig below the surface. Often what is hovering underneath is fear or insecurity or grief, and anger is the way, however unhealthy, that we choose to cope. Yet in the long run, it's not coping at all, because anger doesn't change a situation; it usually makes it worse. In 1639, Thomas Fuller gave some very good advice: "Two things a man should never be angry at: what he can help, and what he cannot help."

If we are serious about overcoming our off-balanced emotions, we first have to find out what is at the root of them. Only then will we be on the road to becoming true instruments of peace.

Often a change in diet can help us deal with anger. In Chinese medicine, each off-balanced emotion is linked to a weakness in a different organ. From this perspective, a toxic liver tends to make people ill-tempered and aggressive. A healthy liver tends to make people patient and thoughtful. We are therefore more susceptible to irritability and anger when we tax our liver by overconsuming drugs, alcohol, caffeine, soft drinks or fatty foods. Experts say that moderating our intake of meat and eating more whole grains and vegetables can also help us be more balanced and slower to anger.

Do I allow myself to indulge in off-balanced emotions?

 What concrete steps can I take to master my energy in motion (emotions)?

 How can I be a greater instrument of peace?

 I strive to walk the Middle Way

Gautama Buddha articulated the initiation of the solar-plexus chakra when he taught that we can make the best spiritual progress by walking "the Middle Way." Gautama learned this lesson first-hand. For six years, he practiced severe austerities and as a result became so weak that he fainted and was believed to be dead.

When he recovered, he realized the futility of excessive and prolonged asceticism. One day, after eating a strengthening meal of rich rice milk, he vowed to sit under a fig tree until he attained enlightenment. He faced many temptations under that tree—temptations he never would have overcome unless his body, as well as his heart, mind

74

and soul, had been strong.

In his first sermon after his enlightenment, given at Sarnath, India, Gautama explained that we can only attain enlightenment by avoiding the extremes of self-indulgence and self-mortification —by walking the Middle Way. In later years he told his disciples, "On a path where one becomes exhausted and weak, one cannot manifest complete Enlightenment." Thus, he articulated one of the most important spiritual precepts of all time: *In all things, strive for balance.*

One hallmark of the Middle Way is tolerance. Its nemesis is fanaticism or extremism, either to the right or to the left. Tolerance means that we accept others as they are because we haven't walked in their moccasins and we don't know the burden they may be carrying. On the other hand, avoiding extremes doesn't mean we are wishy-washy. Our point of balance, our fulcrum, is strong because it is centered in a solid sense of identity and purpose.

Do I remain balanced when pursuing my desires and passions, or do I tend to go to extremes? Do these extremes have a harmful effect on myself or others?

*Is there something that I pursue compulsively
which is preventing me from attaining inner
peace?*

 *Am I easily able to come back to center
when I find myself out of balance?*

 ### I seek to align my desires with my goals in life

We can't have inner peace if we don't master our
desires. This doesn't mean we have *no* desires.
Mastering desire means we tether our desires to the
true desire of our soul and God's desire for us.
When we are able to do that, the momentum of
energy in our solar plexus will propel us toward
the fulfillment of our soul's divine potential.

Our desires, like our emotions, aren't automatically "bad." In his sermon at Sarnath, Gautama
taught that the reason we suffer is that we crave.
Commentators say that the Buddha was trying to
explain that we suffer when our desires are self-
centered or selfish, when they reinforce the human
ego and don't take into account the needs of others.

There is a Buddhist saying about this grasping, possessive part of human nature: "All the harm with which this world is rife, all the fear and suffering that there is: clinging to the 'I' has caused it! What am I to do with this great demon?"

The motive behind our desires is what counts. For instance, if we desire to be educated or to become a doctor or lawyer so we can share the talents God has given us and improve life for others, this is right desire. If this pursuit is based solely on the desire to amass wealth or to control or impress others, that would be a self-centered, inordinate desire.

In other words, there is always the option to fulfill our desires on a higher plane, the plane of service to life. When we opt for that higher plane, when we fuse our free will to the universal will in a dynamic partnership, we can be a dynamo for accomplishing good. That's why a slip of a woman like Mother Teresa could not only work indefatigably but also be a prime mover on the world scene.

The spiritual meaning of the word *desire* is *Deity siring*—God and the presence of God within you giving birth to the highest and noblest aspirations of your soul. Whenever you desire, you are creating (or giving birth to) something. If the energies of your solar plexus are balanced and at peace, the creations born of your desires can be beautiful, powerful and effective.

In fact, we can tell a lot about the condition of our solar-plexus chakra by how effective we are in the arena of action. If we haven't figured out what we really desire—or we have multiple desires that are at fisticuffs with each other—we will not be able to summon the energy or the drive to accomplish our goals. Crosscurrents of desire create confusion and turmoil and cause the energy of the solar plexus to be tied up in knots. It's like an exhausting game of tug-of-war. We don't move forward because we haven't decided which way we're going.

When you don't get confused, your nature is naturally stable; when your nature is stable, energy naturally returns.

—LÜ YEN

Unrest in our solar plexus can be the result of the demands our culture places upon us. The drive for success, wealth or fame may be at odds with our core desires for spiritual growth, soul fulfillment and service to life. One of our challenges at the level of the solar plexus is to free up our energies—to withdraw them from desire that is not God's desire for us—so we can apply the totality of our being to our real goals in life.

Simply put, when our energy is tied up in lesser desires that take us away from our main thrust in life, that energy is not available to invest in the here and now. As a result, we lack vitality and clarity. We spin our wheels and get frustrated.

We master the solar-plexus chakra as we sift through our desires and simplify our life to reflect where we really want to be going. If we don't do this, we may find ourselves the slave of our desires (and our credit card). As the ancient wisdom of the Dhammapada warns us, "Those who are slaves of desires run into the stream of desires, even as a spider runs into the web that it made."

Educational pioneer and visionary George Trevelyan once said that education "has produced a vast population able to read but unable to distinguish what is worth reading." We can say the same of today's "advanced" civilization. It has produced innumerable options for fulfilling our desires, especially with the incredible reach of the media and advertising, but it doesn't teach us to sort through those desires.

Just because we feel the urge to have or to do something doesn't mean it's right for us. We have to distinguish at the soul level whether what we are responding to is God's desire for us or a desire that stems from an unhealthy pattern of the past.

If you find yourself grappling with a desire—"should I or shouldn't I?"—it may be time to take a step back and be honest with yourself: *Why do I want this new _____? Is it a tool to express myself and fulfill my mission, or is it something to adorn my ego? Will it help me be more balanced, or will it take me off on a tangent?*

Another good way to evaluate a desire is to allow a cooling-off period. If you are facing a major decision in life, allow enough time to turn over your desires to God for feedback. Giving a "novena," a certain prayer for a number of days or weeks, can be a helpful ritual. While you are doing this vigil, ask God to reveal to you exactly what the divine will is.

This is especially effective when you use affirmations and prayers that call forth the high-frequency spiritual energy of the violet flame (see pages 87–95). If a desire stems from an unhealthy habit pattern that is holding you back, the violet flame's accelerated energy can help transmute the records of that pattern. You'll find after a number of weeks of directing the violet flame into those conditions that the desire may be gone. Or, if the desire is authentic, the violet flame will help you come to a new understanding of its relevance in your life.

Another key to evaluating desire is perspective. Sometimes pulling away from a situation will give you a reality check. It's like a magnifying glass—if you get too close to something, it's fuzzy. If you pull the magnifying glass away just a bit, then everything comes into focus. Don't be afraid to pull away and take the time you need to make decisions that will have a major impact on your life's direction or your spiritual path.

 *What are my desires giving birth to,
and am I happy with what I have created?*

 *Do I have any crosscurrents of desire that are
keeping my energy tied up in knots? What steps
can I take to resolve these conflicting desires and
free up my energy?*

81

I set aside my own desires when necessary to support and serve others

In a moment of self-reflection, Chief Luther Standing Bear once said, "As a child I understood how to give. I have forgotten this grace since I have become civilized."

The greatest gift you can give is the gift of yourself. God endows us with talents and special qualities so that we can share them with others. We're like God's messengers. We're God's hands and feet on earth, delivering love or comfort, joy or illumination to those he cannot touch physically. "Freely ye have received, freely give," taught Jesus. And the more we give, the more we open up the energy flow. The more we prime the pump, the more that energy flows back to us. That's a principle of abundance, and it works.

We can choose to say, "Here I am, God. You have created me. Use me. Use every aspect of my mind and heart and soul and all of my chakras to manifest your light and your love to everyone I meet!" Or we can become possessive. We can claim the energy that comes to us from our universal Source as our own and stop the flow. When we stop the flow, the energy gets backed up. This creates a downward energy spiral that draws us down into the lesser self rather than a positive energy spiral that sweeps us up into the higher vibrations of spiritual awareness.

A priest once learned a lesson about giving while he was on a retreat. He said of the experience, "There's a monk there who will never give you advice, but only a question. I was told his questions could be very helpful. I sought him out.

Sometimes give your services for nothing, calling to mind a previous benefaction or present satisfaction.

—HIPPOCRATES

"'I am a parish priest,' I said. 'I'm here on retreat. Could you give me a question?'

"'Ah, yes,' he answered. 'My question is, What do they need?'

"I came away disappointed. I spent a few hours with the question, writing out answers, but finally I went back to him.

"'Excuse me. Perhaps I didn't make myself clear. Your question has been helpful, but I wasn't so much interested in thinking about my apostolate

83

[my parish work] during this retreat. Rather I wanted to think seriously about my own spiritual life. Could you give me a question for my own spiritual life?'

"'Ah, I see. Then my question is, What do they REALLY need?'"[4]

What a great question to start every day with.

 What do the people whose lives will intersect with my own today need from me?

 From my storehouse of vitality, what can I give others?

 How can I give back to life the talents and gifts that life has given me?

SPIRITUAL TECHNIQUES

*Affirmations for
Balance and Inner Peace*

Peace, be still! Peace, be still! Peace, be still!

———————

*I AM the hand of God in action,
Gaining victory every day;
My pure soul's great satisfaction
Is to walk the Middle Way.*

———————

The Prayer of Saint Francis

Lord,
Make me an instrument of thy peace.
Where there is hatred, let me sow love;
Where there is injury, pardon;
Where there is doubt, faith;
Where there is despair, hope;
Where there is darkness, light; and
Where there is sadness, joy.
O Divine Master,
Grant that I may not so much
Seek to be consoled as to console,
To be understood as to understand,
To be loved as to love.
For it is in giving that we receive,
It is in pardoning that we are pardoned, and
It is in dying that we are born to eternal Life.

Clearing the Energy Centers

*If the river flows clearly and
cleanly through the proper channel,
all will be well along its banks.*

—LAO TZU

Every moment energy is flowing to us, and every moment we are deciding whether we will put a positive or negative spin on it. By the law of the circle, the law of karma, that energy will return to us. When the positive energy returns (as positive karma), we see positive things come into our life and we have vitality. The energy that has a negative spin on it, because we have used it to harm rather than help others, also returns to us (as negative karma)—this time seeking resolution.

This energy is like debris that collects around our seven energy centers, hampering the natural flow of light and vitality through our body's energy system. When our energy centers and the channels that connect them are clogged, the chakras don't spin at their native frequency or unfold their full potential. We can feel sluggish, pessimistic or sick without even knowing why. When our chakras and the circuits of energy that connect them are clear, we feel more energetic and positive, joyful and giving.

The Karmic Equation

Another way to understand how our past actions affect our life today is to look at the karmic debris surrounding our chakras from the perspective of Feng Shui. Feng Shui is the ancient Oriental art of arranging our external environment to create harmony and balance in our life.

The masters of Feng Shui teach that clutter in our physical environment inhibits the flow of energy (or ch'i) in our surroundings. They say that flow of energy (or lack of it) powerfully affects our health, our finances, our relationships—the very course of our life. In exactly the same way, "karmic clutter" can create blockages in the flow of energy at subtle, energetic levels *within* us, slowing us down physically, emotionally, mentally and spiritually.

Karmic debris is like the leaves that clog up a drain after a storm. In order for the water to run through the drain properly, we must clear away the leaves. Likewise, in order for spiritual energy to flow through and activate our chakras, we need to clear the effluvia that clings to these sacred centers. Just as we wash off the dirt and grime we pick up every day, so we can have a daily ritual of bathing and purifying our chakras.

A High-Frequency Spiritual Energy

The prayers and practices handed down through the world's religions are sacred formulas that call forth the light of the Holy Spirit for purification. In some spiritual traditions, this powerfully transforming energy has been seen as a violet light, known as the violet flame.

Just as a ray of sunlight passing through a prism is refracted into the seven colors of the rainbow, so spiritual light manifests as seven rays, or flames.

When we call forth these spiritual flames in our prayers and meditations, each flame creates a specific action in our body, mind and soul. The violet flame is the color and frequency of spiritual light that stimulates mercy, forgiveness and transmutation.

To "transmute" is to alter, to change something into a higher form. The term was used centuries ago by alchemists who attempted, on a physical level, to transmute base metals into gold—and, on a spiritual level, to achieve transformation and eternal life. That is precisely what the violet flame can do. It is a high-frequency spiritual energy that separates out the "gross" elements of our karma from the gold of our true self so we can achieve our highest potential.[1]

The violet flame also acts like the atmospheric pressure on a barometer. As we call forth the violet flame to consume the debris around the chakras, it presses down. The pressure and acceleration of this light within us causes the Kundalini to rise naturally and nourish the other chakras.

What makes the violet flame such a powerful tool? In our physical world, violet light has the highest frequency in the visible spectrum. Fritjof Capra in *The Tao of Physics* explains that "violet light has a high frequency and a short wavelength and consists therefore of photons of high energy and high momentum."[2] Of all the spiritual flames, the violet flame is closest in vibratory action to the chemical elements and compounds in our physical universe, and therefore it has the greatest ability to interpenetrate and transform matter at atomic and subatomic levels.

You can recite affirmations and prayers to the violet flame as an adjunct to your own spiritual practice. Those of us who have used the violet flame in our prayers have found that it does help resolve patterns of consciousness, dispel inner pain and bring balance into our lives. It creates an awareness and an attunement with the inner self that makes for creativity and a feeling of being alive and well and in action for good on earth.

One woman wrote to me and said, "For years I had consulted with psychologists; they had helped me to see causes, but how could I *change*?" She started working with violet-flame prayers every day and said the violet flame penetrated and dissolved core resentment. "Through the violet flame," she said, "I emerged healthy, vigorous and grateful."

I've seen thousands of people work successfully with the violet flame. It takes a different amount of time—anywhere from a day to several months—for each person to see results. But if you remain constant, you will begin to feel the difference.

I always recommend that those who are new to the violet flame experiment with it. I tell them to give violet-flame prayers and affirmations for at least a month, fifteen minutes a day, and to note the positive changes that start to take place in their life. You can give these affirmations during your morning prayer ritual, while you're in the shower or getting ready for the day, or even as you travel to work, do your errands or exercise.

You can use the "Chakra Affirmations" in this section to purify and energize your chakras so that you can experience the highest levels of your spiritual potential.[3] These affirmations start with the central chakra, the heart chakra, and move in a spiral action through the chakras above and below the heart.

SPIRITUAL TECHNIQUES

Chakra Affirmations

I AM a being of violet fire,
I AM the purity God desires! *

My heart is a chakra of violet fire,
My heart is the purity God desires!

I AM a being of violet fire,
I AM the purity God desires!

---

*Each set of affirmations is typically given at least three times or
in multiples of three.

My throat chakra is a wheel of violet fire,
My throat chakra is the purity God desires!

I AM a being of violet fire,
I AM the purity God desires!

My solar plexus is a sun of violet fire,
My solar plexus is the purity God desires!

I AM a being of violet fire,
I AM the purity God desires!

My third eye is a center of violet fire,
My third eye is the purity God desires!

I AM a being of violet fire,
I AM the purity God desires!

My soul chakra is a sphere of violet fire,
My soul is the purity God desires!

I AM a being of violet fire,
I AM the purity God desires!

My crown chakra is a lotus of violet fire,
My crown chakra is the purity God desires!

I AM a being of violet fire,
I AM the purity God desires!

My base chakra is a fount of violet fire,
My base chakra is the purity God desires!

I AM a being of violet fire,
I AM the purity God desires!

FOURTH ENERGY CENTER:
HEART

LOCATION: center of chest

COLOR: pink, rose

SANSKRIT NAME: Anahata ("unbeaten" or "unbroken")

PETALS: 12

POSITIVE EXPRESSION: love, compassion, beauty, selflessness, sensitivity, appreciation, comfort, creativity, charity, generosity

UNBALANCED EXPRESSION: hatred, dislike, selfishness, self-pity, human sympathy, negligence

PART OF BODY: heart, thymus, circulatory system

MUSICAL INSTRUMENT: harp

GEMSTONE: ruby, diamond, garnet, rose quartz, pink beryl

SPIRITUAL TRADITION: Christianity

The heart fires of loving-kindness and charity impel us to wise and compassionate action

HEART CHAKRA

LIFE LESSON:
Become Love
in Action

*The important thing is not
to think much but to love much;
and so do that which best stirs you to love.*

—TERESA OF AVILA

The heart center is the most important energy center in the body. It is the hub of life, physically and spiritually. Just as oxygenated blood from our lungs is pumped by the heart to the rest of the body, so the energy we receive from God passes through our heart chakra before it moves on to nourish the other chakras and systems of our body.

As energy passes through your heart chakra, it takes on its imprint—the unique vibration and quality of your heart. "As [a man] thinketh in his heart, so is he," says Proverbs. If the motive of our heart is pure and we are intent upon giving love, kindness and compassion to others, then the energy flowing through our heart chakra will go forth to bless and energize.

If, on the other hand, the energy that emits from our heart chakra is impure—if it is tainted with selfishness, hatred or dislike—all of our chakras can suffer. That's why it's so important to begin our meditations and spiritual practices by clearing and balancing the heart.

A lot of people today talk about centering in the heart, speaking from the heart, acting from the heart. But there are some misconceptions about

My strength is as the strength of ten because my heart is pure.

—GALAHAD
IN "SIR GALAHAD"

what that looks like. Real love is not sentimental or passive. It is strong and it is soft. And, as the mystics tell us, it is eminently practical.

The Sufi poet Rumi, for instance, wrote, "Someone asks, How does love have hands and feet? Love is the sprouting bed for hands and feet!"[1] Mother Teresa would have agreed with this wholeheartedly, for out of her love was born an all-consuming service to others. Love, for her, was an essential part of the drama of everyday life. "We do no great things," she explained. "We do only small things with great love."

The mystic and saint John of the Cross said the goal of life, our ultimate union with God, can only be achieved through this "living flame of love." Because the heart center and its love fires are so essential to our physical, emotional and spiritual vitality, the initiations and lessons that involve the heart are some of the most profound we will ever encounter.

I cultivate compassion

What is true compassion? In order to answer that question, we have to make a distinction between compassion and sympathy. We tend to use those words interchangeably, but in order to understand the subtleties involved in developing the heart chakra, it helps to make this distinction: Compassion comes from the level of our Higher Self and gives to another what he or she really needs in that moment. Sympathy comes from the level of the lower self and stands in the way of what the soul really needs.

Sympathy allows us to feel sorry for ourselves, to indulge our weaknesses, to slide into a "woe is me" slump. Sympathy validates that sense of victimization rather than helping us see our challenges as opportunities. In the aura, sympathy shows up as a syrupy dripping of energy from the heart and as spirals of energy moving downward, which eventually drag down the emotions and soul awareness as well.

Compassion, on the other hand, dips into the pure fires of the heart to uplift others so they can realize their full potential. Compassion supports the process of soul refinement. Compassion doesn't leave someone who is hurting where it finds him.

It's okay to support a child, a friend or a loved one, but when our caring cushions them from learning their lessons and growing from them, we aren't doing them any favors. Sometimes those we love the most need a dose of reality, a wake-up call.

There is another difference between compassion and sympathy. Sympathy can be overbearing or smothering rather than supportive. We can't force a flower to blossom by pulling apart its leaves or by overwatering it. But we can make sure it has enough (and not too much) air, water, sunlight, food—the right environment and the right nutrients. Having done that, we can only let go and allow the flower to unfold according to its own inner timetable and inner strength. The same thing applies to the souls in our care.

Letting go is sometimes so hard. When our children are first beginning to walk, we want to guard them from getting hurt and give them the support they need. Yet it's so essential to let them try and try again until that first step is entirely their own. The same is true for all the steps we take in life. No one can do it for us, and we can't do it for anyone else.

 Do I tend to provide compassion in the form of support and realism, or do I give sympathy by indulging or smothering?

 Am I able to let go when I need to and let others take their own steps forward?

How can I turn sympathy into compassion more often in my life?

I look at challenging circumstances as opportunities to keep my heart open

There are two universal truths that we sometimes forget.

Number one: Not everyone thinks, feels and acts like we do.

Number two: It's *okay* that everyone doesn't think, feel and act like we do.

We don't have to be on a crusade to change anyone. We don't have to share Henry Higgins' sentiment, "Why can't a woman be more like a man?"—Why can't he/she be more like me?

One of the most important things we can teach children at an early age is to enjoy people's differences. Give people room to be who they are. We're going to meet all kinds of people in the world who may not fit our mold. But more often than not, they have something to teach us. No matter who comes your way, try to keep your heart open and uncover what God wants you to learn from them, because there are no mistakes. Life brings us into contact with the people and situations we need.

While the philosopher and spiritual teacher

Gurdjieff led a community in France, one of the people who lived there was an irritable and unkempt old man. He did not fit in well with the group, and nobody got along with him either. Even the old man seemed to realize this and after several difficult months he left for Paris. Gurdjieff followed him and asked him to change his mind, but the old man refused to go back to such an

I follow the religion of Love: Whatever way love's camel takes, / That is my religion, my faith.

—IBN ARABI

unpleasant situation. At last, Gurdjieff offered the man a substantial pension to rejoin the community.

When the ornery fellow reappeared on the scene, the other community members were astounded. And when they found out that Gurdjieff was paying him—while they were actually paying Gurdjieff to live in the community—they became even more upset.

Finally Gurdjieff explained why he just could not let the man go away. "If he wasn't here, you wouldn't learn what you need to learn about anger or about compassion," he told them. "That's why you pay me, and why I pay him!" This wise teacher knew that the crabby old man was the fine grain of sand, the irritant, that would create the shining pearls in his community.

Don't you think God does the same thing? He "arranges" things so we can learn about anger, irritability, patience and compassion. When we have an instant dislike for someone, we've probably bumped into our karma. And the faster we face that karma and resolve it with love, the faster we're going to be liberated from it. "Be grateful for whoever comes," advised Rumi, "because each has been sent as a guide from beyond."[2]

Whisper a prayer to God to help you stay openhearted and to show you exactly what you are supposed to learn from the situation. Call to your Higher Self and to the Higher Self of the other person to direct your relationship. Then simply be kind and let the rest unfold.

In the short run, it may seem easier to ignore a situation, rebel against it or run away. But in the long run, it isn't. When we dislike someone, we tie ourselves to them. Remember the scene from *Return of the Jedi*? Luke Skywalker is trapped with the evil emperor and Darth Vader. The emperor is trying to lure Luke to the Dark Side. At one point, the emperor turns to Luke and taunts him with these words: "The hate is swelling in you now. Take your Jedi weapon. Use it. I am unarmed. Strike me down with it. Give in to your anger. With each passing moment, you make yourself more my servant."

Luke realizes that his hatred will tie him to the Dark Side. He centers in his heart, reaffirms his allegiance to "the Force," and ultimately—by his own love—draws Darth Vader back to the Light. But the emperor was absolutely right: Hatred brings us to the feet of the object we hate.

 What are the challenging situations in my life, and what am I supposed to learn from them?

 Are there circumstances in my life right now that I can look at as opportunities to keep my heart open? What can I do to keep compassion alive in these situations?

I acknowledge and appreciate the spiritual beauty in myself and others

Many of us weren't brought up learning how to coach. Our role models were managers, not mentors. It's part of our collective challenge in this new millennium, in this age of Aquarius, to nourish and express our caring feminine side—the side of ourselves that has to do with building relationships, coaching, team work.

A good starting point is to simply go out of the way to appreciate others. Every day, go up to someone and thank her for her contribution—whether it's the good work she did or just the fact that she is so cheerful and sunny. The more we reinforce the positives in others, the more likely they are to repeat that positive behavior. And the more we reinforce their negatives, the more likely they are to believe that that is all they are capable of and therefore repeat that same behavior.

In addition, the more we learn to love and appreciate ourselves, the more love we will magnetize into our world. "A loving person lives in a loving world. A hostile person lives in a hostile world," said Ken Keyes, Jr. "Everyone you meet is your mirror." In down-to-earth terms, Lucille Ball once said, "I have an everyday religion that works for me. Love yourself first and everything else falls into line. You really have to love yourself to get anything done in this world."

The spiritual activity of our heart has definite effects on our health and vitality. Researchers at the Institute of HeartMath, for instance, have shown that emotions like anger and frustration put a strain on the heart and other organs. Emotions like love, compassion and appreciation have the opposite effect: they create harmony in the body that leads to enhanced immunity and improved hormonal balance.[3]

There's a wonderful Hasidic tale that shows the tremendous effect that appreciation can have, not only on ourselves but on the world around us. Every so often, a rabbi would retreat into a small hut in the woods surrounding a monastery. One day the abbot of the monastery visited the rabbi and asked his advice. He explained that his order was shrinking—so much so that only five monks lived there, and they were all over seventy.

The rabbi told the monk that he was experiencing the same problem. Fewer and fewer people were coming to the synagogue. "I'm afraid I don't have any advice," the rabbi said. "I can only tell you that one of you is the Messiah."

Upon returning home, the abbot told the other four monks what the rabbi had said. Could one of them really be the Messiah? they wondered. Although each of the monks had his little quirks, they began to see that each had great virtue as well. Because any one of them could be the Messiah, they carefully treated one another with greater appreciation and respect. And they began to value and respect themselves too.

Only from the Heart can you reach the sky.

—RUMI

Once in a while, the people of the town would enjoy picnics on the beautiful grounds of the monastery and sometimes meditate in its old chapel. As the months went by, the people began to feel something special. There was a certain ambience around the place because the monks treated each other with such reverence.

So the townspeople started coming back more often to visit. They brought their friends with them. Eventually some of the younger men who visited the monastery started talking to the monks. First one and then another of the young men asked to join the order. By the time a few years had elapsed, the monastery was full and it had become a center of great spirituality—all because of the rabbi's parting words of wisdom to the abbot and the power of appreciation.

The healing power of our hearts can indeed create a chain reaction. In his Hopi message to the United Nations in 1992, Thomas Banyacya said, "If we return to spiritual harmony and live from our hearts, we can experience a paradise in this world."

Liu I-ming, a Taoist who was born around 1737, said that the power to change the world does begin within each of us. He wrote, "A sage said, 'If for one day you can master yourself and return to considerate behavior, the whole world will return to humanity.' Do you think humanity depends on yourself or on others? This is indeed the subtle point of this passage."[4]

 Do I look for ways to appreciate others?
Do I go out of my way to give others credit
for their contributions?

Do I look for ways to appreciate myself?

 If I am given the opportunity to lead or to guide, do I use it to encourage the creativity of others rather than to fulfill my agenda? Do I use the role of leader to manage others or to coach?

 ## I set healthy boundaries

Just as one of the initiations of the heart is to keep it open, another is to draw healthy boundaries. Yes, you are allowed to say no!

If we cannot set limits when necessary, it is actually unhealthy—not only for us but for others. When you say yes to everything, you know how easy it is to become overextended and exhausted, irritable and uncreative. If we don't take enough time or space to recharge and nurture ourselves, we are that much less effective in fulfilling our mission. To truly help others, we need to pay attention to ourselves first.

Setting healthy boundaries also means that we can stand up for our principles in the face of peer pressure or societal pressure. It means we can say no to those things that will not propel us toward our ultimate goals in life.

Twentieth-century Trappist monk and writer Thomas Merton once pointed out that even in a spiritual setting peer pressure can be a problem: "The poorest man in a religious community is not necessarily the one who has the fewest objects assigned to him for his use.... Often [he] is the one who is at everybody else's disposition. He can be used by all and never takes time to do anything special for himself."[5] Rabbi Moshe Leib expressed the same sentiment: "A human being who does not have a single hour of his own every day is no human being at all."

There is a Buddhist story about a young woman who learned an important lesson about boundaries from her Buddhist meditation master. Each day she would concentrate on developing loving-kindness in her heart. But as soon as she left the house for the market she would have to deal with a merchant who met her with unwelcome advances. Finally, she lost her cool and, brandishing her umbrella, chased the impudent shopkeeper down the street.

Unfortunately, her meditation master was watching her from the side of the street. She approached her teacher, ashamed that she had lost her temper. In his most gentle tone, he told her, "The next time something like this happens, fill your heart with as much loving-kindness as you can—and then take your umbrella and hit this rogue right over the head!"

There does come a time when we have to draw the line for the protection of our own energy and chakras—and we can usually do it without hitting someone over the head with our umbrella! At times I've had to learn my lessons in drawing boundaries the hard way. Someone once called me on the phone and became irate with me. After I hung up, I could literally feel a pain in my heart, and it took me some time to recover. I later realized that the most loving thing I could have done, both for me and the person on the other end of the phone, was to draw my boundaries by politely saying good-bye and hanging up.

The soul is not where it lives but where it loves.

—THOMAS FULLER

When people are angry, we do have the option of explaining to them softly but firmly that we will be happy to talk to them later, when they are feeling better, but we will have to conclude the conversation if they continue to talk in this manner. We can't always change someone else, but we can take responsibility to guard our own energy by drawing healthy boundaries.

 Are there circumstances in my life where I need to draw healthy boundaries for myself?

 In these situations, how can I lovingly communicate these limits?

I recognize the power of softness

Both Eastern and Western adepts tell us that the greatest power in the universe is softness. Lao Tzu used the analogy of water: "There is nothing softer and weaker than water, and yet there is nothing better for attacking hard and strong things.... The weak overcomes the strong and the soft overcomes

113

the hard.[6]... The softest, most pliable thing in the world runs roughshod over the firmest thing in the world."[7]

When water is running through your fingers it doesn't feel "strong," and yet water can wear down rock and find pathways in, through and around gigantic obstacles. The power of softness can do the same.

Softness is a receptive mode where unnatural, forceful human actions and reactions give way to the natural movement of the heart. Softness is a nurturing, giving attitude that does not take offense. Softness is the opposite of brittleness, rigidity or resistance. Brittle things can break, but softness is flexible and can bend. As a wise commentator once said, "Blessed are the flexible, for they shall not be bent out of shape."

That's the whole principle behind the martial arts, such as T'ai Chi Ch'uan. They are based on cultivating inner energies and developing softness that will triumph over the use of external, muscular force. The body appears to be soft and gentle externally but has a great concentration of internal power.

The twentieth-century T'ai Chi Ch'uan grand

master Cheng Man-ch'ing writes: "Those who love combat never fail to use stiff and brutish force to strike their opponents, or fast techniques to grapple with them.... If one's defense against this is hard, the result will be defeat and injury for both parties. This is not mastery.

"If my opponent uses hardness, I neutralize it with softness. If my opponent attacks with movement, I meet him with stillness.... This is what Lao Tzu referred to as softness and weakness overcoming hardness and strength."[8]

Through the heart, all mankind are one.

—DJWAL KUL

In our personal interactions, softness is a gentle way of dealing with a situation that doesn't degrade the other person (or yourself) but shows him that you have his best interests at heart. Take this example from Zen Buddhism. A student studying meditation with a Zen master would sneak over the temple wall at night and run into town to have some fun.

The master discovered this one night when he noticed the stool the student was using to make his getaway and return. So one night the master waited in the cold and stood in the place where the stool usually was. When the student returned, he stepped onto his teacher's head and jumped to the ground. When he realized what had happened, he was shocked and embarrassed.

"It's quite cold this time of the morning," his teacher simply said. "Take care so you don't catch cold." The student never again resorted to a midnight escapade. His master's single act of softness changed his life.

 Are there times when I have seen softness rather than harshness turn around a situation, and what can I learn from this?

 The next time I find myself in a charged situation, how can I use softness to turn it around?

SPIRITUAL TECHNIQUES

The Heart Affirmation

Experiences in this life and past lives can create a burden on the heart. Sometimes these experiences cause us to close our heart. We become guarded because we have been hurt and we don't want to be hurt again. Sometimes our heart is burdened because we have been selfish or angry or hard-hearted. When we use the energy of the heart in unloving ways, that energy remains with us as part of our consciousness until we transmute it by love.

The following heart affirmation has helped many people attune with their loving heart. It creates a spiritual climate around the heart that helps us become more open, more sensitive and more compassionate to ourselves and to the plight of so many who need our love and our prayers.

This affirmation invokes the alchemy of the

violet flame to clear the painful records of past experiences. It helps clear our subconscious, which accepts the wrong judgments of peers or authority figures who have put us down or intimidated us. The violet flame can resolve these patterns of consciousness and free us to be our real self.

The heart affirmation is easy to remember and you can give it aloud (or under your breath) any time things aren't going well or you feel a heaviness around your heart. You can recite it once, three times or a hundred times as you go deeper and deeper into meditation and visualization.

Visualization:

As you recite the heart affirmation, visualize the violet flame within your heart chakra as a pulsating violet light that softens and warms your heart. See it melt away layers and layers of encrustation around the heart.

As the violet flame saturates your heart chakra, feel it transforming anger into compassion, bitterness into sweetness, anxiety into peace. See the twelve petals of your heart center unfold as your heart radiates its native energy of divine love.

Heart

Violet fire, thou love divine,
Blaze within this heart of mine!
Thou art mercy forever true,
Keep me always in tune with you.

Meditation on the Light of the Heart

The more we focus on the heart and the qualities of heart in our life and in our spiritual practices, the more powerful and sensitive our heart will become. The beautiful prayer "I AM the Light of the Heart" by Saint Germain celebrates the divine spark within our hearts and can help us become more heart-centered.

Visualization:

As you recite "I AM the Light of the Heart," visualize radiant light descending from God into your heart chakra, where it will be released according to the words of your prayer.

Then focus your attention on your heart chakra, in the center of your chest. Sometimes it's easier to focus your attention if you place the thumb and first two fingers of your hand in the center of your chest.

Now picture the brilliance of the sun at noonday and transfer that picture to the center of your chest.

See thousands of sunbeams going forth from your heart to penetrate and dissolve any darkness, despair or depression within yourself, within loved ones and then within the people of the world. Project your love (which is really God's love) out into the world.

See that love going forth as intense fiery-pink laser beams that break down all barriers to the success of your relationships, your family, your spiritual growth, your career, your neighborhood or your nation.

I AM the Light of the Heart

I AM the light of the heart
Shining in the darkness of being
And changing all into the golden
  treasury of the mind of Christ.

I AM projecting my love
Out into the world
To erase all errors
And to break down all barriers.

I AM the power of infinite love,
Amplifying itself
Until it is victorious,
World without end!

FIFTH ENERGY CENTER:
THROAT

LOCATION: throat

COLOR: blue

SANSKRIT NAME: Vishuddha ("pure" or "purify")

PETALS: 16

POSITIVE EXPRESSION: power, will, faith, protection, direction, courage, obedience

UNBALANCED EXPRESSION: control, condemnation, idle chatter, gossip, human willfulness, impotence, cowardice, doubt

PART OF BODY: thyroid, lungs, respiratory system

MUSICAL INSTRUMENT: brass

GEMSTONE: diamond, sapphire, star sapphire, lapis lazuli

SPIRITUAL TRADITION: Judaism

By mastering will and power, we release the elevated energies of the heart through the spoken word for personal and world transformation

May we have your comments on this book?

We hope that you have enjoyed this book and that it will occupy a special place in your library. It would be helpful to us in meeting your needs and the needs of our readers if you would fill out and mail this postage-free card to us.

Book title: _____

Your comments: _____

_____

_____

_____

How did this book come to your attention? _____

How would you rate this book on a scale of 1 to 10, with 10 being the highest? _____

Topics of interest to you: _____

Would you like to receive a free catalog of our publications? ☐ Yes ☐ No

Name _____ Address _____

City _____ State _____ Zip Code _____ Phone no. _____

(We will not make your name available to other companies.)

E-mail: _____

Thank you for taking the time to give us your feedback.

Call us toll free at 1-800-245-5445. Outside the U.S.A., call 406-848-9500. Summit University Press titles are available from fine bookstores everywhere. E-mail: tslinfo@tsl.org

491-YSEC 8/02

SUMMIT
UNIVERSITY
PRESS®

*Publisher of fine
spiritual books
since 1975*

THROAT CHAKRA

LIFE LESSON:
Summon Inner
Power to Create
Constructive Change

*Better than a thousand useless
words is one single word that gives peace.*
—THE DHAMMAPADA

The throat chakra is our power center. At this level, we have the ability to coalesce through the spoken word what is in our minds and on our hearts. The sages of East and West tell us that the spoken word holds the key to creating change. Genesis, for instance, recounts that the process of creation began when "God *said,* 'Let there be light.'" Through the throat chakra, we can become co-creators with God.

The sages of East and West also say the mastery

of the throat chakra is central to our spiritual growth. That mastery involves not only what we say but how we say it—and what we choose not to say.

 I practice right speech

Every single time we open our mouths we are making a choice: to help or to harm. Jesus explained that our words are of ultimate import when he said, "By thy words thou shalt be justified, and by thy words thou shalt be condemned [judged]." That's because our words come from our power center and therefore have incredible impact. When we think back to the moments in our life that were the most traumatic and the most meaningful, they often involved what someone said to us or about us.

Right speech is a major precept of Buddhism. It is one of the keystones of Gautama Buddha's Eightfold Path that leads to liberation. In essence, right speech means that we guard the flow of energy through our throat chakra and realize the impact it has on others. It means we look at our ability to speak as a gift that God has given us to convey compassion, kindness and teaching.

Gautama taught that the one who espouses right speech does not bring division through gossip but uses his speech to create harmony and unity. "What he has heard here he does not repeat there, so as to cause dissension," the Buddha said. Instead, such a one "delights in concord" and "brings together those that are at variance." He or she "has given up harsh language. . . . He speaks words that are free from rudeness, soothing to the ear, loving, going to the heart, courteous, . . . elevating many."[1]

Power is not revealed by striking hard or often, but striking true.

—BALZAC

Theosophist C. W. Leadbeater says that at energetic levels our words, even in casual speech, are much more potent than we realize. "Many people think that in daily life it is not necessary to take the trouble to speak clearly," he writes. "It matters much more than they think, because we are all the time building our own surroundings, and these react upon us."

125

He explains that if someone becomes depressed, for example, his room "becomes charged with that quality, and any sensitive person coming into it becomes conscious of a certain lowering of vitality, a loss of tone." In the same way, "the man who surrounds himself with unpleasant sound-forms by careless and uncultured speech produces an atmosphere in which these forms constantly react upon him."

In fact, says Leadbeater, "each word as it is uttered makes a little form in etheric matter, just as a thought does in mental matter." He says the word *hate,* for instance, "produces a horrible form, so much so that, having seen its shape, I never use the word. We may say that we dislike a thing, or that we do not care about it, but we should never use the word 'hate' more than we can help, for merely to see the form that it makes gives a feeling of acute discomfort.... It is surely better that we should surround ourselves with beauty than with ugliness, even though it be in etheric matter."[2]

Leadbeater wrote this in 1925 and said that someday he believed "all this might be worked out scientifically."[3] Until that day, he said that as a general rule of thumb, words connected with desirable qualities produce pleasant forms, and those associated with negative qualities produce ugly forms.

The lessons of the throat chakra are closely related to our ego and to our solar plexus. If we have a chip on our shoulder, it is all too easy to allow hurt feelings at the level of the solar plexus to percolate up and arc to the throat chakra. It happens so fast, we don't even realize it. That's why the sages advise us to short-circuit that emotional response. Slow down and think about the effect your words will have before you open your mouth, they urge. "Let every man be swift to hear, slow to speak, slow to wrath," warns the Book of James. "Good people should be slow to speak but quick to act," says Confucius.

Right speech is supportive speech, kind speech, respectful speech. Someone who understood this very well was America's first president. In the nineteenth century, a school notebook of George Washington's was discovered at Mount Vernon, Washington's home. It seems that in 1745, the fourteen-year-old George had written in this notebook more than one hundred "Rules of Civility in Conversation Amongst Men," which he had copied from a work that dated back to 1664 or earlier.

These "rules of civility" are a delightful guideline for right speech. Here are just a few of them:

"In the presence of others sing not to yourself with a humming voice, nor drum with your fingers or feet. Speak not when others speak, sit not when others stand, and walk not when others stop."

"Be no flatterer, neither play with anyone that delights not to be played with."

"Let your discourse with men of business be short and comprehensive."

"Be not hasty to believe flying reports to the disparagement of anyone."

"Utter not base and frivolous things amongst grown and learned men, nor very difficult questions or subjects amongst the ignorant, nor things hard to be believed."

"Deride no man's misfortunes, though there seem to be some cause."

"Think before you speak; pronounce not imperfectly, nor bring out your words too hastily, but orderly and distinctly. When another speaks, be attentive yourself and disturb not the audience."

"Whisper not in the company of others."

"Labor to keep alive in your breast that little spark of celestial fire called conscience."[4]

128

Do I think about the impact of my words on others before I speak?

 Do I use my speech to create harmony and unity?

I recognize the value of silence

One of the subtlest forms of imbalance in the throat chakra is idle chatter. "Those who have virtue have something to say, but those who have something to say do not necessarily have virtue," observed Confucius.

Gautama taught that the person who has mastered right speech "bears in mind the injunction which says: 'In meeting one another, Brothers, there are two things that ought to be adhered to: either conversation about the Truth or holy silence.'"

Idle chatter or argumentation is an obstacle to our self-mastery because it drains our energy. It fritters away the vitality of our power center. If we speak only when we need to speak, we preserve our vitality. The Tao Te Ching bluntly describes the

129

"strong silent type" who has mastered that prescription: "Those who know do not talk. Those who talk do not know.... Keep your mouth shut, guard the senses, and life is ever full. Open your mouth, always be busy, and life is beyond hope."[5]

This doesn't mean that we should never say anything. Gautama, for instance, said that the one who has mastered right speech "speaks at the right time, speaks in accordance with facts, speaks to the point."[6] There is a time to speak and a time to remain silent. One practical rule of thumb is that if what you are going to say doesn't add something of value to a conversation, why say it?

The Quakers build their worship meetings around this entire principle. When they come together to worship, they take their seats and wait in silence. Placing themselves and their affairs in the presence of God, they open their minds and hearts to the divine Spirit. If someone feels moved by the inner Spirit to say something, he does so without anyone interrupting him. Those who listen receive with charity what is said and the spirit behind what is said.

The American Quaker Rufus Jones, born in 1863, witnessed to the wonder of these silences and the words of power they gave birth to. He wrote, "We never ate a meal which did not begin with a hush of thanksgiving; we never began a day without 'a family gathering' at which mother read a chapter of the Bible, after which there would follow a weighty silence."

These silences, wrote Jones, were important features of his spiritual development. "There was work inside and outside the house waiting to be done, and yet we sat there hushed and quiet, doing nothing. I very quickly discovered that something real was taking place. We were feeling our way down to that place from which living words come, and very often they did come. Some one would bow and talk with God so simply and quietly that He never seemed far away.

I have often regretted my speech, never my silence.

—ANONYMOUS

"The words helped to explain the silence. We were now finding what we had been searching for. When I first began to think of God I did not think of Him as very far off."

How powerful and authentic our words can be when they have first been steeped in the silence of our spirit. As Anne Morrow Lindbergh once said, "A note of music gains significance from the silence on either side."

 Do I allow myself to remain silent if I have nothing valuable to say at the moment?

 Do I take time to get in touch with my inner spirit before I speak?

I stand up for and speak the truth

Gautama Buddha taught that a person who embraces right speech "speaks the truth, he is devoted to the truth, he adheres to the truth, he is worthy of confidence."[7] Speaking the truth involves speaking the facts without distortion. It means not exaggerating and not jumping to conclusions. It means overcoming passivity to stand up for what we know is right, regardless of what others think. "You do not need to justify asking questions," historian Jacob Neusner once said. "But if you think you have found answers, you do not have the right to remain silent."

On the subject of exaggerating, my father had this habit when he was telling stories—and he loved to tell stories. So I too developed that habit when I was young. Later, my spiritual teachers called me on that. They taught me that exaggeration is little more than a lie because it is a misrepresentation of the facts. They also taught me that it is important never to make a promise if there's a chance you won't be able to keep it. These seem like small details, but they make a world of difference in our interaction with others.

It can be quite an interesting exercise to note how many times during the day you deviate from the truth—even if it's just by a millimeter. It is even more interesting to figure out why. Is it just a habit pattern? Is it a sense of insecurity or fear or concern about what other people will think of you?

Confucius once said that by being honest and by supporting those who are honest, we can raise up an entire nation. "Promote the honest, placing them over the crooked," he said, "and you can cause the crooked to straighten out.... If leaders are trustworthy, people will not dare to be dishonest.... It is said that if good people work for a country for a hundred years, it is possible to overcome violence

133

and eliminate killing. This saying is indeed true."[8]

Children imitate those they look up to—and so do adults. Each one of us is a role model for someone. We reflect the inner workings of our hearts and souls to those around us through our speech patterns—by what we don't say, what we do say and how we say it.

 *Do I consistently speak the truth,
or do I exaggerate at times?*

*Do I make assumptions and speak
before I know the facts?*

*Can I be depended on to speak up when
I need to?*

 ## I exercise the power of the spoken word for transformation

Just as there is a time to speak and a time to remain silent, there is a time to meditate and a time to take the fruit of our meditation and send it forth in the science of the spoken word. The creative power of sound is at the heart of the world's spiritual traditions East and West, whether as the Jewish Shema and Amidah, the Christian Our Father, the Muslim Shahadah, the Hindu Gayatri or the Buddhist Om Mani Padme Hum.

Hindu yogis have used mantras for protection and wisdom, to enhance their concentration and meditation, and to help them achieve enlightenment and oneness with God. In Jewish mystical tradition, Kabbalists taught that by calling and meditating on the names of God, we could tap into an infinite source of power to restore peace and harmony to this world. In Catholic tradition, the rosary and other prayers are repeated to invoke divine intercession.

Both scientists and sages tell us that the spoken word can literally create change and transformation. For instance, Dr. Herbert Benson, president and founder of the Mind/Body Medical Institute at Harvard Medical School, found that those who repeated Sanskrit mantras for as little as ten minutes a day experienced physiological changes—reduced heart rate, lower stress levels and slower metabolism.

Subsequent studies showed that repeating mantras can benefit the immune system, relieve insomnia, reduce visits to the doctor and even increase self-esteem. When Benson and his colleagues tested other prayers, including "Lord Jesus Christ, have mercy on me," they found that they had the same positive effect. In short, repetitive prayer energizes.

In terms of our chakra initiations, prayer and affirmation can also provide a boost to our personal growth because they can help us undo the false mental programming that may be lodged in our subconscious. Our subconscious is like a recording machine. It records every impression we have absorbed throughout our life and our past lives—the good and the bad. And, to our detriment, that includes the negatives we have heard and believed about ourselves.

Every time you think something negative about yourself, every time someone criticizes or intimidates you, your subconscious records the event. Sometimes we don't realize how much we've been influenced by another's thoughts or words, especially a parent, sibling or authority figure. These negatives are booby traps that can undermine our success. All too often we limit ourselves—our job, our income, our educational level, our goals in life—by what we believe about ourselves.

The subconscious not only records negative impressions but, like a tape player on automatic replay, it plays back the recordings of the past. That's why positive affirmations have been found to be so helpful. When used properly, they can help us align our subconscious as we affirm the innate beauty and positive potential of our soul.

Handle them carefully, for words have more power than atom bombs.

—PEARL STRACHAN HURD

I have had the best results in clearing the subconscious of negatives by using mantras and affirmations to the violet flame. You can ask your Higher Self to direct the violet flame into the specific thoughts, actions and words that produced the negative recordings in your subconscious. Visualize the violet flame literally burning up these records, one by one.

Stephen Covey in his best-selling *Seven Habits of Highly Effective People* says that affirmations and visualizations can be extremely helpful. He reminds us that "in effective personal leadership, visualization and affirmation techniques emerge naturally out of a foundation of well thought through purposes and principles that become the center of a person's life." He says these techniques "are extremely powerful in rescripting and reprogramming" as we seek to align our life with the purposes and principles that are most important to us.[9]

Affirmations, especially those using "I AM," are a potent form of spoken prayer. I AM affirmations use the name of God "I AM" to access spiritual power. "I AM" comes from "I AM THAT I AM," the name God revealed to Moses when he said, "This is my name forever, and this is my memorial unto all generations."[10] The Jerusalem Bible translates this passage as "This is my name for all time; by this name I shall be invoked for all generations to come."

What does "I AM THAT I AM" mean? To me it means simply but profoundly "as above, so below." God is affirming, "I am here below that which I AM above." When you say, "I AM THAT I AM," you are affirming that God is where you are. In effect, you are saying: "As God is in heaven, so God is on earth within me. Right where I stand, God is. I am that 'I AM.'"

138

In an I AM affirmation, you are summoning the inner power of your throat chakra and God's power within you to bring about constructive change. You can create your own short, powerful I AM affirmations, tailored to your own needs, such as "I AM forgiveness acting here," "I AM the light of the heart," or "I AM the power of peace." I AM affirmations are generally given with determination and power.

Every time we say, "I AM _____ ," we are really saying, "God in me is _____ ." And whatever we affirm following the words "I AM" will become a reality in our world—whether we say "I am sick," "I am tired," "I am having a great day" or "I am healthy." This is because the state of our body is influenced by what we think and by what we say. The light of God flowing through us will obey our direction. Simply put, *spoken words command energy. The creations of our powerful throat chakra are self-fulfilling prophecies.*

When you come to the place where you realize that the tremendous energy of God is flowing through you every moment, you begin to have a sense of reverence and awe. You say to yourself, "Here is God's energy. What will I do with it today? Will I use God's energy to reinforce the negative side of life? Or will I use it to affirm something beautiful, something real, something that matters to my spiritual progress and that benefits others?"

 What circumstances have I created in my life by affirming either negatives or positives about myself?

 What are the negative beliefs I have about myself that undermine my success in life?

 How can I incorporate into my life the power of the spoken word through prayers, affirmations or mantras to transmute these negatives?

SPIRITUAL TECHNIQUES

*Affirmations for the
Throat Chakra*

Lo, I AM come to do thy will, O God!

---

*I AM life of God-direction,
Blaze thy light of truth in me.
Focus here all God's perfection,
From all discord set me free.*

*Make and keep me anchored ever
In the justice of thy plan—
I AM the presence of perfection
Living the life of God in man.*

SIXTH ENERGY CENTER:
THIRD EYE

LOCATION: between the eyebrows

COLOR: emerald green

SANSKRIT NAME: Ajna ("to command")

PETALS: 96 (or 2)

POSITIVE EXPRESSION: truth, vision, holding the highest vision of myself and others, healing, wholeness, abundance, clarity, constancy, focus, music, science

UNBALANCED EXPRESSION: falsehood, lack of vision, mental criticism, lack of clarity, inconstancy, spiritual impoverishment

PART OF BODY: pituitary (or pineal), portions of the brain

MUSICAL INSTRUMENT: piano

GEMSTONE: emerald, diamond, jade, quartz crystal

SPIRITUAL TRADITION: Confucianism

*By focusing our inner vision
on the divine plan, we achieve
clarity and creative insight*

THIRD-EYE CHAKRA

LIFE LESSON:
Sustain a Vision
of Wholeness for All

The light of the body is the eye.
If therefore thine eye be single,
thy whole body shall be full of light.

—JESUS

Through the sixth energy center, the third-eye chakra, we can access the power of inner vision to perceive the reality of a situation. In addition, the third-eye chakra, as well as the crown chakra, connects us with the magnificent realm of the higher mind and its flashes of insight, genius and originality.

An insight is an *in-sight*, a looking within. The word *insight* means the power of seeing into a situation, into oneself or into the inner nature of things. It is discernment and penetration. The third eye is also associated with intuition, which comes from the Latin word meaning to look at, to contemplate. Our insights and our intuitions are the interior revelations that come to us through the third-eye chakra when we are in tune with our Higher Self.

You must trust that small voice inside you which tells you exactly what to say, what to decide. Your intuition is your instrument.

—INGMAR BERGMAN

These revelations can come as hunches, promptings or even as visions. Many times, if God wants me to do something or know something, I find that he will put a picture in front of me. I will literally get a "vision"—an image—of what I need to do.

When we access the pure power of our third eye, we have clear perception and a clear perspective on life. Through the third eye, we hold in mind the highest blueprint and the best outcome for a situation. We tune into what should be (the divine pattern) instead of what is now happening, and we have the discrimination to know what is the truth and inner reality of a situation.

The seat-of-the soul and third-eye chakras are closely linked. Speaking about the energies of the soul raised to the third eye, the adept Djwal Kul says, "While the outer man takes life at its face value, the soul is evaluating the flow of energy, of karma, and of the cycles of life from the standpoint of inner reality. . . . The image and likeness of God . . . out of which male and female were created, is held in the third eye of each one as the potential that every living soul is destined to fulfill."[1]

Thus our challenge at the level of the third eye, he says, is to purify this energy center so that we can anchor the perfect pattern of our being in outer form and focus our concentration on the upper reaches of our highest self.

I honor the creative genius and insights that come to me and others

Honoring the creative insights that come to us is one way we master the energies of the third-eye chakra. This requires setting aside our analytical thinking and judging to allow space for the flashes of genius that can come our way.

Detailed analysis and evaluation is an important and necessary skill. But if we overanalyze, we can dampen the creative fires. That's why creative writing courses encourage us not to filter our work before getting it on paper. Just sit down and write, they advise, because if you critique your words before you get them out, they may never escape from the prison-house of your mental judgment.

We have a responsibility to ourselves and to others to let both sides of the brain have their say—the creative side and the logical side. We've probably all experienced a time when we've been so excited about a new idea that we couldn't wait to share it with a friend or partner or parent. But instead of simply listening and encouraging, they started analyzing the idea and telling us why it may or may not work: "Have you thought about this or considered that?"

These questions are a valid part of the next step, but they are not always helpful or appropriate when the creative juices are flowing. Remember how you went away feeling as if someone had just dumped a bucket of cold water on your fire? That's a dangerous situation to be in. In the long run, if we take it too personally, these kinds of situations can keep us from feeling good about ourselves and from accepting the bursts of imagination and originality when we get them.

Another trap we have to watch out for is the ironclad judgments of our own human intellect. Our lower mind will try to convince us that the unusual idea that just came into our head is not feasible—or that it's even downright stupid. Don't allow yourself or anyone else to dismiss your inspirations and insights as "just your imagination." In fact, as soon as these ideas pop into your head, write them down. Hang on to them.

"The fierce power of imagination is a gift from God," said the twentieth-century Kabbalist Abraham Isaac Kook. "Joined with the grandeur of the mind, the potency of inference, ethical depth, and the natural sense of the divine, imagination becomes an instrument for the holy spirit."[2]

Napoleon Hill in *Think and Grow Rich* stresses the importance of "creative imagination" to achieve our goals. He says that only a small number of people deliberately use their faculty of creative imagination. "Those who use this faculty voluntarily, and with understanding of its functions, are geniuses," he says. "The faculty of creative imagination is the direct link between the finite mind of man and Infinite Intelligence. All so-called revelations, referred to in the realm of religion, and all discoveries of basic or new principles in the field of invention, take place through the faculty of creative imagination."

Hill goes on to say that "one of America's most successful and best-known financiers followed the habit of closing his eyes for two or three minutes before making a decision. When asked why he did this, he replied, 'With my eyes closed, I am able to draw upon a source of superior intelligence.'"[3]

Some of the most ingenious inventions have come from the creative imagination and inspiration of our third eye. Velcro, for instance, was developed in the 1940s when the Swiss inventor George de Mestral went on a walk with his dog and noticed afterwards that his pants and his dog's coat were covered with cockleburs. His curiosity (or was it a higher inspiration?) led him to study the burrs under a microscope. He discovered their natural hook-like shape. This became the basis for the creation of Velcro.

Imagine if George's wife had told him to just go clean off his pants and stop babbling about that crazy new idea of his. He may never have had the confidence to pursue his hunch.

 Do I honor new ideas, whether from myself or others, or do I sometimes short-circuit the creative process with my analytical mind?

 Have the opinions of others dampened my creative genius over the years? If so, what steps can I take to make time and space in my life to encourage those inspired visions?

I recognize that what I put my attention on, I will become

When Jesus said, "If therefore thine eye be single, thy whole body shall be full of light," he was talking about the single-eyed vision of the third-eye chakra. He was talking about the truth that where our attention rests, so will the light/energy of our being. When the eye is "single"—when it is focused on God, on good, on the highest potential—we open a tremendous highway of light between our world and the divine world.

With all the details of our day, how often do we remember to place our attention upon God, upon good, upon that highest potential? Taking even a short time-out during our daily routine to focus with our third eye on the inner light, on God, on our highest goals, can make an incredible difference. For whatever we place our attention on, we energize. More than that, whatever we place our attention on, we become. Gautama Buddha summarized it best when he said, "We are what we think, having become what we thought."

Dr. Charles Garfield has shown that peak performers, including exceptional athletes, all use the power of visualization. They actually visualize themselves meeting their targets. They are using the power of their third eye, their inner eye, to focus their attention. And what they put their attention on, they become. We can do the same.

In order to be perfection, man must see perfection.

—DJWAL KUL

Dr. Wayne Dyer, for instance, says that what we really, really, really, really want, we will get. And what we really, really, really, really *don't* want, we will get too—because whatever we put our energy into will come to pass. Just think about what Job said: "The thing which I greatly feared is come upon me, and that which I was afraid of is come unto me."

"Attention is the key," says Saint Germain. "Where man's attention goes, there goes his energy." And where our energy goes, creation will follow. The corollary to this is where our attention *doesn't* go, where we withdraw our energy, *dis*integration will follow.

A scene from the television special *Merlin* captured this concept wonderfully. In that version of Merlin's story, Queen Mab is the architect of evil. Her sole aim is to control King Arthur and Merlin. She instigates the birth of Modred and rears him from the time he is a child to be the enemy of Arthur. But when both Modred and Arthur die at each other's hands, her plans go awry.

In one of the final scenes, Queen Mab and Merlin face off. Merlin holds his own against Queen Mab's magical powers, but it's not easy. As she continues to taunt him, Merlin finally announces to Mab that she has absolutely no power over him or over the knights of Camelot because they are simply going to "forget" her.

He and the knights turn their backs on Mab and walk in the other direction. She screams out and demands that Merlin look at her, but neither Merlin nor the knights heed her plea. Alone and without a single adversary—no one to support her or to fear her—she slowly disintegrates into nothingness. She cannot exist unless someone believes she is real.

These concepts have great significance for our lives and our chakra development. If we want to develop mastery in a certain skill or virtue, we must put our attention on it *and* we must withdraw our attention, our vision, from what does not contribute to our success.

Because our vision and our thoughts have the power to create, I've always encouraged women who are pregnant to meditate on classical music and beautiful works of art to convey patterns of beauty and perfection to the soul of their unborn child. Mothers- and fathers-to-be can make a meditation book with pictures of flowers, beautiful scenes from nature, angels and the Madonna and child. Mothers-to-be can run their fingers over the lines of a statue of David by Michelangelo to transfer to the fetus that archetypal form of perfection.

It's also a good idea to actively use the power of your inner vision in your spiritual practices. Whenever you meditate or pray, you will get greater results if you visualize the outcome of what you are praying for. See it taking place before your eyes. See the details of those goals as if you were already at the finish line—a new job or home, a loving relationship, the healing of a loved one.

🌸 *Can I remember a time when I have put my attention on something positive (or not so positive) and therefore magnetized it into my life?*

🌸 *Is there something in my life right now that I need to focus on more fully? Is there something I need to withdraw my energy from because it is interfering with a creative endeavor?*

I strive to recognize and overcome mind-sets and to see as God sees

When we have single-eyed vision, when we place our attention upon God, we allow our eye to

153

become God's eye. We see what God sees. We see *as* God sees.

What often keeps us from seeing as God sees is our fixed mind-sets, our stereotypes. A mind-set is a "set mind." A Zen adept once said: "Stop talking, stop thinking, and there is nothing you will not understand.... There is no need to seek Truth: only stop having views." The views he's talking about are our mind-sets. The more rigid they are, the less chance there is for God, or anyone, to bring us a new way of seeing something, a new insight.

Have you ever noticed how hard it is to be creative and inspired when people with rigid minds are around? Someone with a strong mental concept about something is like a barbed-wire fence. That's why master alchemists, like Saint Germain, tell us it is not a good idea to share all our plans with even our closest friends.[4] People's mind-sets or closed minds can spoil our creative endeavors and stop us from tapping into our higher mind. The severe misuse of the energies of the third-eye chakra to harm or spoil another's plans is what some refer to as the "evil eye."

Mark Prophet talked about the danger of mind-sets and stereotypes in a lecture he gave called "Educating Your Vision." Mark said, "What are stereotypes? Well, people will look at someone and say, 'This person looks like my Aunt Mamie. And my Aunt Mamie thinks this way, and therefore this person must think this way.'

"One of the errors we're prone to fall into is looking at people and making up our mind about them. When we make up our mind about another person, we have a tendency to literally put an iron kimono around them. And the first thing you know, our rigid ideas about them become their experiences and they wonder why they are acting that way."

Mark goes on to tell the story of a certain Mr. Wright, who had been his employer. This distinguished gentleman had a way of projecting certain stereotypes (certain mind-sets) onto his employees: "This one is efficient. That one is inefficient." He had them pigeonholed. Whenever Mr. Wright would come near Mark, Mark would start to have terrible feelings of inferiority. He would begin to stutter, even though he never stuttered around anyone else.

As Mark said, people tend to put others in a box—and never let them out: "They want to say,

At one time she was this. At one time he was that. The last I knew of him he was a drunkard or a dope addict or God only knows what." Instead, encouraged Mark, "let us allow people the freedom to express the higher aspects of themselves rather than confine them to some prison cell of our own creation."

 What mind-sets or stereotypes am I holding onto about myself? About others?

 Do I try to see others as God sees them?

 I practice holding in mind the highest image of others, even though they may not be manifesting it now

Through the inner vision of your third eye along with the intuition of your soul chakra, you can tap into the "immaculate concept" for your life, your projects, your plans. The immaculate concept is the divine blueprint for what is meant to be. When we hold this concept in mind with constancy, when we focus our energy and inner vision there, we will create the image we are "seeing" and it will come into being.

We can hold this blueprint in mind not only for our own life but for others. Just as God continually holds the perfect image for us, so we can hold that image for others. As Goethe once said, "If you treat men the way they are, you never improve them. If you treat them the way you want them to be, you do."

At a practical day-to-day level, holding the immaculate concept for someone means that we don't jump to conclusions before we know the facts. It means that we allow ourselves and others the opportunity to transcend what we might have been decades ago, weeks ago or even an hour ago. Recognizing our misperceptions can be challenging. We don't always perceive things as they actually are, because what we take in goes through the filter of our own emotional and mental matrix.

The Burmese political dissident Aung San Suu Kyi has talked about this. If you saw the movie *Beyond Rangoon*, she was the woman who bravely walked toward a row of soldiers whose rifles were poised to shoot her. The soldiers were in such awe of her courage that they didn't touch her. She was under house arrest in Burma for six years and was released in 1995, but is under strict government control in the Burmese capital, Rangoon.

In a country where thousands of political prisoners are detained and tortured, Aung San Suu Kyi fearlessly speaks out for democracy and is a devout Buddhist. In the book *The Voice of Hope*, compiled from conversations with Alan Clements, she spoke about cultivating "awareness," which relates to the initiation of the third-eye chakra.

Lo, I am with you always *means when you look for God, God is in the look of your eyes, . . . nearer to you than your self.*

—RUMI

She said that the search for truth "is in a sense the struggle to overcome subjectivity" as we learn to distance ourselves from our prejudices when assessing a situation.

"The search for truth," she said, "has to be accompanied by awareness. . . . If you are aware of what you're doing, you have an objective view of yourself. And if you are aware of what other people are doing, you become more objective about them too.

"For example, awareness means that when you are aware of the fact that somebody is shouting, you don't think to yourself: 'What a horrible man.' That's purely subjective. But if you are aware, you know that he's shouting because he's angry or frightened. That's objectivity. Otherwise, without awareness, all kinds of prejudices start multiplying."[5]

In another conversation, Aung San Suu Kyi said that humor can help us develop objectivity. The interviewer had expressed how shocked he was that on the day she was placed under arrest, she and her assistants "all just laughed about the crisis and started cracking jokes."[6] On another occasion, the persecuted leaders of the democracy movement in Burma laughed to the point of tears at the absurdity of the behavior of the Burmese military intelligence, who had just interrogated one of them for twenty-seven hours nonstop.

Aung San Suu Kyi replied: "Obviously, it's not a happy situation we're in, but the seriousness of the situation is something we can all joke about. In fact, lots of Burmese people joke about it; there are jokes about forced labor, about prison....I think a sense of humor requires a certain amount of objectivity in the situation, which is why it's so healthy.

"If you see things as a whole, you can always see a humorous side of it. Which is why we laugh at situations which to some seem so serious. I mean, when U Win Htein and others were laughing at his account of the interrogation, if you see it as a whole it's quite ridiculous. But if you see it from just one angle, it could be infuriating, humiliating, or even frightening for some people."[7]

 Do I jump to conclusions when dealing with certain people or situations?

 Do I hold the highest image for myself, my family, my partner, my co-workers?

SPIRITUAL TECHNIQUES

*Affirmations for
Balancing the Third Eye*

Visualization:

Take some deep breaths. Focus your energy at the point of your third-eye chakra, between your brows.

See your third-eye chakra as a pulsating energy center of intense emerald green. (If you start to feel uncomfortability or pain between your brows, gently move your concentration to your heart.)

Once you have mastered this visualization, you can then visualize something you want to see take place—the achievement of a goal, the resolution of a situation at work, the improvement of a relationship. As you do, repeat the following affirmations:

I AM, I AM beholding all,
Mine eye is single as I call;
Raise me now and set me free,
Thy holy image now to be.

I AM the eye that God does use
To see the plan divine;
Right here on earth his way I choose,
His concept I make mine.

SEVENTH ENERGY CENTER:
CROWN

LOCATION: crown

COLOR: yellow, gold

SANSKRIT NAME: Sahasrara ("thousandfold")

PETALS: 972

POSITIVE EXPRESSION: illumination, wisdom, self-knowledge and Self-knowledge, understanding, humility, cosmic consciousness, open-mindedness

UNBALANCED EXPRESSION: intellectual and spiritual pride, vanity, intellectualism, ego-centered-ness, narrow-mindedness, ignorance

PART OF BODY: pineal (or pituitary), cerebral cortex, nervous system

MUSICAL INSTRUMENT: strings

GEMSTONE: yellow diamond, yellow sapphire, topaz

SPIRITUAL TRADITION: Buddhism

Through knowledge of the inner Self, we attain wisdom (wise-dominion), enlightenment and oneness with all life

CROWN CHAKRA

LIFE LESSON:
Create Unity
out of Diversity

I am a part of all that I have met.
—ALFRED, LORD TENNYSON

The seventh energy center, the crown chakra, is where we receive and experience wisdom and enlightenment. The opening of this center in the full radiance of its golden-yellow light has been depicted as the halo of the saints. It has also been portrayed as the vibrant corona around the Buddhas and the dome-shaped or flamelike protuberance on top of their heads.

The wisdom of the saints and the Buddhas is not knowledge of the things of this world. It is knowledge of the reality that lies *beyond* the physical world—the inner reality that enlivens the outer form. The wisdom of the crown chakra tells us that more important than all our intellectual prowess is our knowledge of this inner reality.

When Gautama Buddha was asked, "Who are you?" he answered, "I am awake." To be enlightened means that we are awake to our inner potential. When we are awake, we understand the limitations of our lesser self and the limitless resources of our greater Self.

Through our crown chakra, we can connect with a higher source of knowledge—our own higher mind, one with the mind of God. We can tap into our own creative genius. For a genius, as Napoleon Hill observed, is simply one "who has discovered how to increase the intensity of thought to the point where he can freely communicate with sources of knowledge not available through the ordinary rate of thought."[1]

The wisdom of the crown, inextricably linked with compassion, impels us to share what we have received with those who need it most. After Gautama Buddha meditated under the Bo tree and attained enlightenment, he entered nirvana for forty-nine days. Then, before he could impart to others the wisdom he had gleaned, the Temptress, Mara, tried to convince Gautama to return to nirvana. There was no use sharing his experience, said Mara, because no one would understand it. But Gautama did not turn back. He simply responded, "Some will understand."

In one way or another, we are all called to share the enlightenment we have received along life's path. The wisdom we glean from our higher intelligence, from the universities of the world or even from the school of hard knocks is a gift. Out of our compassion for others we are compelled to share that gift—whether we use it to guide the children in our family or neighborhood, develop a computer program that will help others learn new skills, or heal the sick.

I strive to reach beyond the limitations of the human intellect

Pablo Picasso once said, "Computers are useless. They can only give you answers." As for the questions that fly beyond the borders of the known—

they are what catapult us into the realm of genius. Cambridge cosmologist Stephen Hawking tells us, "There is no prescribed route to follow to arrive at a new idea. You have to make the intuitive leap."

One of the secrets of the crown chakra is that this leap in consciousness does not require a doctorate. Having a well-developed human intellect does not necessarily qualify us to access the divine intelligence. In fact, Lao Tzu said, "Without going anywhere, you can know the whole world. Without even opening your window, you can know the ways of Heaven. You see: the further away you go, the less you know."

The purpose of learning is to grasp the divine.

—ABRAHAM ABULAFIA

By educating ourselves, we can prepare ourselves to receive the impulses of our higher mind and the mind of God in our chosen profession. But the intellect is not the mind of God. As Ralph Waldo Emerson said, "A man should learn to detect and watch that gleam of light which flashes across his mind from within, more than the lustre of the firmament of bards and sages."

In fact, our education can even get in the way at times, especially if it is a breeding ground for pride. We have to be willing to bypass the concepts of the intellect that would reason away God's concepts.

That's the modus operandi of the Zen masters and their koans, or riddles. One Zen master explained, "Those who seek the truth by means of intellect and learning only get further and further away from it. . . . Not till you abandon all thoughts of seeking for something, not till your mind is motionless as wood or stone, will you be on the right road to the Gate."

Bill's story illustrates this point. A computer programmer, Bill says that sometimes the programs he writes are so complicated he hits a mental block. "Sometimes I think, this is beyond my expertise. I just can't do it," he says. "But if I can become centered and put myself in a position of being a chalice for God to work through, then from some place in cosmos—I don't know where —a thought comes into my head that wasn't there before.

"It tells me to look at a certain thing. Then that leads to something else that leads to something else—and I arrive at the answer. But in order to get there, I have to get rid of the feeling of being inadequate to the task and open up."

Tapping into our own higher intelligence can give us the answers we can't find anywhere else. Sometimes we're a little bit like Pope John XXIII. He once joked, "It often happens that I awake at night and begin to think about a serious problem and decide that I must tell the pope about it. Then I wake up completely and remember that I am the pope!"[2]

When you wake up in the middle of the night looking for the answer to a problem, don't forget that you have unlimited access to all the knowledge and creativity you need—*if* you are prepared to receive it.

Do I tend to rely too much on my human intellect, or do I try to tap into my higher creative mind?

When I receive insights and inspiration that can help others, do I share them?

I take time to slow down, still my mind and spend time in solitude

One way we can balance our crown chakra and prepare to receive the impulses of the divine intelligence is to slow down and still the outer mind. Are you able to quiet your mind? Are you easily distracted? Do you occupy your mind with trivialities or fantasies? To paraphrase the Taoist sage Chuang Tzu, "If you cannot keep your mind still, that is called galloping even while sitting."

Does your mind gallop even while you're sitting? It's not an uncommon problem. In the eighth-century classic called *The Guide to the Bodhisattva's Way of Life,* the poet-monk Shantideva compares the unwieldy mind to a mad elephant. "It is not possible to observe any discipline without guarding the quivering mind. Unsubdued and overwrought elephants do not effect that damage here which the unrestrained mind, an elephant running wild, does." If the sluggish mind is fixed on something else, he says, then all our spiritual practices, even if we engage in them for a long time, "are useless."[3] Again, that's because where our attention goes, there goes our energy.

171

Our minds and bodies are interconnected. So in order to still the mind, we need to care for our body. It's easier to concentrate and focus when we get enough sleep and exercise and when we take in foods and substances that strengthen us rather than those that weigh us down (like too much oil) or make us jittery (like too much salt or coffee).

Another way to bring balance to our crown chakra is to make time for meditation and communion with God. Take time to study your favorite scriptures or inspirational works. Take time to receive the revelations that God wants to give you personally. Spend time alone.

Sometimes we fill up our day with so many activities that we forget to listen for the inner voice of wisdom. When you look over your schedule for the week, pencil in some priority time for yourself before your hours get filled up.

One time I was talking to someone about scheduling a meeting. He said, "We'd better mark it down on our calendars right now, even if it's three weeks away, because my time gets filled up so fast." Then he shot me a glance and said, "I do the same thing with my wife." He turned a couple pages of his calendar to two months from that time and said, "See, I'm meeting with my wife on the twentieth at 8 P.M. She wanted to make an appointment with me to be *sure* I would have time set aside to talk to her in the next two months."

That's how it is in our society today. We're moving so fast that we have to *make* time for the special people in our lives. Two of those special people are you and God.

Sometimes when we get depressed or out of sorts, it's because we aren't spending enough time away from the madding crowd. When the soul is not allowed to follow her natural inclination toward union with God, the yearning for that union becomes a loneliness that even the greatest human relationships cannot fill.

In 1953 and 1954, Thomas Merton was able to devote some special moments to solitude and meditation, and he wrote down his thoughts on solitude and the contemplative life. Merton discovered that we do not have to be "perfect" for God to share his wisdom with us. "Only solitude," wrote Merton, "has taught me that I do not have to be a god or an angel to be pleasing to You [God], that I do not have to become a pure intelligence without feeling and without human imperfection before

You will listen to my voice. You do not wait for me to become great before You will be with me and hear me and answer me."[4] These are the sweet revelations and breakthroughs you can have if you take time to be alone with God.

And don't always be so quick to share your most intimate sacred experiences with others. "God does not tell his purest secrets to one who is prepared to reveal them," observed Merton. "He has secrets which He tells to those who will communicate some idea of them to others. But these secrets are the common property of many. He has other secrets, which cannot be told. The mere desire to tell them makes us incapable of receiving them."[5]

There are certain spiritual experiences that are holy and need not be shared with others. Mark Prophet once said, "I think one of the greatest mistakes people make is telling their neighbor or their friends or their companion some of the spiritual experiences that have come to them. A lot of times these companions will say to you, 'Oh, that's wonderful! That's so sweet.' Then they'll turn around and say, 'You know, I think she's getting a little bit senile!'"

Do I spend enough time in solitude?

 During my day, do I consciously try to slow down, still my mind and attune to my higher mind?

I embrace the unity underlying the diversity

At the level of the crown chakra, the thousand-petaled lotus, we are initiated in the highest wisdom and the highest understanding—the knowledge that there are not two, but one.

There are not two—you and I. There are not two—you and God. There is only one: There is only God. There is only Spirit. There is only Self, with a capital *S*. The rest is illusion.

This is the mystery that the mystics and adepts have unlocked. We can know it intellectually, but until we understand it with all of our heart and soul and mind, we are still living in a sense of duality—two, not one. As long as we operate from a perspective of duality, we have not yet integrated with the highest energies of the crown chakra.

Rumi expressed this truth in a simple parable about the human ego, which has a hard time identifying with the true Self and with God. It goes like this. Someone once knocked at the door of his Friend. "Who's there?" asked the Friend. "It's me," came the answer. But the Friend told him to go away because there wasn't room for raw meat at his table.

Instead of being so bound up with everyone, be everyone.

—RUMI

After a year, the person returned—completely cooked—and knocked again. "Who is it?" asked the Friend. "You," came the answer this time. The Friend opened the door, explained there was only room for one in his house—and then invited him to enter.

When we understand that there are not two but just one, then God will share all of himself with us—because we have shared all of ourselves with God.

One of the oldest renditions of this mystic theme can be found in the Upanishads, the ancient Hindu scriptures. In a conversation between the young man Nachiketas and Death, Death promises

Nachiketas three gifts. First, the young man asks to be reconciled with his father. The second gift he asks for is the fire that leads to heaven. For his third gift, he asks Death to explain what happens to a man after death.

In the course of their conversation, Death slowly unveils the secret of immortality. He says: "Some have never heard of the Self, some have heard but cannot find Him.... Logic brings no man to the Self.... That boundless Power, source of every power, manifesting itself as life, entering every heart, living there among the elements, that is Self.... Tell the mind that there is but One."

Death goes on to explain that Nachiketas should not look for this "Self" outside of himself. This indwelling Spirit, says Death, is "that Person, no bigger than a thumb, burning like flame without smoke, maker of past and future." This inmost Self, he reveals, is God—who "lives in the heart."[6]

The Spirit that dwells within us is described in many of the world's religions. In Hindu tradition, the Katha Upanishad also speaks of the "light of the Spirit" that is concealed in the "secret high place of the heart" of all beings. Buddhists speak of the "germ of Buddhahood" that exists in every living being. Christian theologian and mystic Meister Eckhart taught that "God's seed is within us." There is a part of us, he wrote, that "remains eternally in the Spirit and is divine. . . . Here God glows and flames without ceasing."

When we begin to identify less with the outer man, the ego, and more with that Person in the heart—the one who burns "like flame without smoke"—then, and only then, are we on our way to the full flowering of our crown chakra.

As the energies of our crown become more accelerated and balanced, we are able to sustain an abiding sense of oneness with Spirit while we walk the earth. And we are able to recognize that Spirit within everyone.

When the energies of the crown are unbalanced, we aren't able to sustain an awareness of the indwelling Spirit that is our essence. Or, at the other extreme, we may let our spiritual experiences "go to our head" as we convince ourselves that we are better than others. Or we may bask in spiritual bliss, in our own spiritual ivory tower, and never come down to earth. But this is not the path of the crown chakra. The initiation of the crown demands that we let go of our pride, our ego, our aloofness and find a way to make our spirituality *practical* and all-embracing.

The negative vibrational quality of pride can energetically create a murky, dark corona around the head rather than the brilliant yellow corona of the illumined ones. This dark energy can obliterate our contact with the higher mind, making it even harder to receive the impulses of the divine through the crown chakra.

The rite of passage that we face at the level of the crown chakra also demands that we appreciate others and learn from everyone. One of the signets of the emerging new spirituality of our era is an appreciation of diversity. As we move forward into the future, we can learn much from a giant of the past—Akbar the Great, the sixteenth-century Mogul emperor.

[The Yogi] sees himself in the heart of all beings and he sees all beings in his heart.

—THE BHAGAVAD GITA

Akbar was a great military genius and a wise ruler, the greatest ruler of his time. But above all, his burning desire was to reconcile the diversity of religious creeds that he saw before him—Christian,

179

Muslim, Hindu, Zoroastrian and Jewish. He was the first monarch in the medieval age to recognize that truth existed in all religions. How many people of the world, even today, acknowledge that?

Akbar saw the seed of truth in all religions. As a result, he actually created his own monotheistic, unitarian religion, called Divine Faith. His goal was to bring about unity amid diversity. As I've studied the mystical paths of the world's religions, I've come to realize that these paths are much, much more alike than they are different. That's the way it is with so many things in life. And we can enjoy the diversity—and even benefit from it—while seeking the underlying unity.

 Do I honor diversity and try to learn from it?

 Do I seek to find the common bond that can bring me and others together, or do I dwell on our differences?

SPIRITUAL TECHNIQUES

Affirmations for Activating the Crown Chakra

Through our crown chakra, we receive the creative thoughts of God and our Higher Self. The following affirmations can help clear the physical and spiritual faculties of the mind. They can help you strengthen your intuitive faculties and develop a keener perception of spiritual dimensions.

As you give these affirmations, see the violet flame clearing your mind of all mental blocks, negative images and limiting concepts about yourself or others. See your mind becoming filled with the brilliant golden light of the crown chakra.

Crown Chakra Meditations

O flame of light bright and gold,
O flame most wondrous to behold,
I AM in every brain cell shining,
I AM light's wisdom all divining.
Ceaseless, flowing fount
*   of illumination flaming,*
I AM, I AM, I AM illumination.

I AM light, thou Christ in me,
Set my mind forever free;
Violet fire, forever shine
Deep within this mind of mine.

God who gives my daily bread,
With violet fire fill my head
Till thy radiance heavenlike
Makes my mind a mind of light.

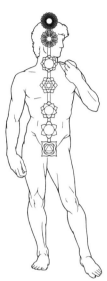

Sealing Your Chakras

When vitality passes into the eyes, the vision is clear; when it is in the ears, the hearing is sharp. When it is in the mouth, speech is accurate; and when it gathers in the mind, thought is penetrating.

—HUAI-NAN-TZU

Your energy centers (chakras) are the spiritual organs that govern the flow of energy within you, affecting your vitality, your outlook on life and your spiritual growth. The perpetual flow of energy that moves as a river of light through your chakras will keep your body, mind and spirit in a positive spin. The lack of energy flow, like air trapped in a stuffy room, can create stagnation, depression and even disease.

Sometimes, even though we don't realize it, we

aren't able to hold on to our energy. When this happens, we can feel drained and lose our zest for life. There are many ways this can happen in each of the different chakras. As I've said, we can lose energy if we feed it into negatives—a negative outlook about ourselves or others, anger, agitation, gossip, excessive chatter, hatred, jealousy.

We can also experience an energy drain when we get into a spiritually unhealthy environment. For example, sometimes when we interact with someone who is glum, we begin to feel sad ourselves. Just by being in a crowd or in a big shopping mall, we can get exhausted and out of sorts. This happens simply because that which has a lesser vibration than our own will drink in our energy, as the parched earth absorbs water, unless we are protected.

When you start to feel something or someone pulling on your energy, that's when you can turn to your spiritual toolbox. The "Tube of Light" affirmation and "Meditation for the Sealing of Your Chakras" on the following pages can help you reestablish your equilibrium and connect with your loving Higher Self.

Your Spiritual Anatomy

Each of us has a personal connection with God through our Higher Self. The Chart of Your Divine Self facing page 186 can help us understand this relationship. It is a diagram of your spiritual anatomy and your potential to become who you really are. Author Dannion Brinkley, who has had three near-death experiences, says, "This is what you look like from spiritual realms."

The upper figure in the chart is the I AM Presence, the personal Presence of God that is individualized for each of us. Buddhists call it the Dharmakaya, or the body of Ultimate Reality.

The middle figure represents your Higher Self —your wise inner teacher, chief guardian angel and dearest friend. Some call the Higher Self "the inner Christ" or "the inner Buddha." Each of us is meant to become, right here on earth, the reflection of our Higher Self by manifesting the full potential of our spiritual nature.

The shaft of light that descends from the heart of the I AM Presence to the lower figure is the crystal cord, the umbilical cord that connects you to your spiritual Source and nourishes your energy centers. The lower figure, representing you on the spiritual path, is enveloped in the purifying spiritual energy of the violet flame and the protective white tube of light, which you can call forth in your spiritual practices.

The Chart of Your Divine Self

The White Light

The saints and mystics have seen and felt the white light in their prayers and meditations. The Israelites, for instance, experienced the tube of light as a "pillar of a cloud" by day and "a pillar of fire" by night as they journeyed through the wilderness. And God promised through the prophet Zechariah: "I will be unto her [Jerusalem] a wall of fire around about, and will be the glory in the midst."

The white light can help you stay centered and at peace. It guards you from negative energies that may be directed at you through someone's anger, condemnation, hatred or jealousy. When you have a strong forcefield of light around you and within you, the light will reject and repel the negativity. When you are unprotected, those aggressive energies can make you irritable or depressed. They can even cause you to have accidents.

SPIRITUAL TECHNIQUES

Meditation on the White Light

You can summon the protective white light through the "Tube of Light" affirmation. The tube of light is a shield of energy that descends from God through your Higher Self in answer to your call.

It's best to give the "Tube of Light" affirmation each morning before the hustle and bustle of the day begins. If throughout the day you feel de-energized, depleted or vulnerable, withdraw for a few minutes and repeat this affirmation.

Visualization:

As you recite the "Tube of Light" affirmation, see dazzling white light, brighter than the sun shining on new-fallen snow, descending from God. See it coalesce to form around you an impenetrable wall of light about nine feet in diameter, shielding you from all negativity.

Inside this scintillating cylinder of light, see yourself enfolded with the violet flame. From time to time throughout the day, you can reinforce this spiritual protection by visualizing the white light around you and repeating this affirmation.

Tube of Light

Beloved I AM Presence bright,
Round me seal your tube of light
From ascended master flame
Called forth now in God's own name.
Let it keep my temple free
From all discord sent to me.

I AM calling forth violet fire
To blaze and transmute all desire,
Keeping on in freedom's name
Till I AM one with the violet flame.

After you give this affirmation as many times as you wish, you can give the "Meditation for Sealing Your Chakras" on the next page to protect your energy centers from absorbing the off-balanced energies that may come to you in the course of the day.

Meditation for Sealing Your Chakras

You can repeat the following meditation throughout the day whenever you feel the need to energize or seal your centers. As you practice this meditation, you will develop a sensitivity in your seven chakras and in the centers of your palms. Although your chakras are positioned along your spinal column, for the purposes of this exercise you will always be moving your right hand to the corresponding position along the front of your body.

Heart chakra

1. Place your left hand over your heart chakra, in the center of your chest. (Keep your left hand there throughout the meditation.) Place your right hand on top of your left hand.

Visualize a fiery white disc in your heart. See your right palm pulling out this white light, which you will now use to nourish each chakra.

Feel the spiritual fire intensifying in your heart chakra. Feel the warmth of the love that is in your heart intensifying.

Crown chakra

2.   Leaving your left hand over your heart chakra, place your right hand over the top of your head, one to two inches above your crown chakra. You are drawing energy from your heart chakra with your left hand, and with your right hand you are placing this energy over your crown chakra.

Close your eyes and visualize this white-fire disc of God's energy charging, stimulating and balancing your crown chakra. See and feel the connection of light as the light flows through your right palm to your thousand-petaled, golden crown chakra. To activate the flow of light, slightly rotate your right hand clockwise.

Third-eye chakra

3.   When you feel that you have made contact with the intensity of light moving into your crown chakra, move your right hand to about an inch in front of your third-eye chakra, between your eyebrows.

Visualize the white-fire disc in your right hand spinning over your third eye. Rotate your right hand clockwise over your third-eye chakra. See this 96-petaled chakra, an intense emerald green, and feel the energy of the white light activating your third eye.

You can do this for shorter or longer periods of time, depending on how long you want your meditation to be. If you feel any pain in your third eye, move to the next step so as not to overstimulate the chakra.

Throat chakra

4.   When you are ready, move your right hand to an inch in front of your throat chakra, at the base of the neck. Visualize the disc of dazzling white fire activating your throat chakra as you rotate your right hand in a clockwise direction. See and feel this 16-petaled chakra, an intense blue, as it is energized, purified, balanced and healed.

Heart chakra

5.   With your left hand still in the center of your chest over your heart chakra, move your right hand to an inch over your heart chakra. Feel the light charging your heart chakra as you rotate your hand. Feel the light intensifying through the 12 petals of this radiant pink chakra. You can take several deep breaths.

193

Solar-plexus chakra

6. Move your right hand to an inch over your solar-plexus chakra, at the point of the navel. The light now invigorates this 10-petaled, purple-and-gold chakra, known as the "place of the sun."

Feel the white light going into this chakra, establishing inner peace as you rotate your right hand in a clockwise direction. Let go of all that is not peace in your life—any friction, worry, unresolved problems. Again, take some deep breaths as you allow the light to stabilize the solar plexus and restore it to its native harmony.

Seat-of-the-soul chakra

7. Move your right hand to an inch in front of your seat-of-the-soul chakra, midway between the navel and the base of the spine. This is where your

194

soul dwells until she has balanced her karma and moved to the level of the heart. Your soul is sensitive, intuitive, fragile. Your soul is your inner child.

Visualize the dazzling white disc over your 6-petaled soul chakra, violet in color. As the light continues to enter this chakra, see it embrace your inner child—soothing, comforting and strengthening. Rotate your right hand in a clockwise direction to intensify the action of the light.

Base-of-the-spine chakra

8. Move your right hand to an inch in front of your base-of-the-spine chakra. Rotate your right hand in front of this four-petaled, white center to seal, stimulate and balance its energies.

Base to the crown

9. Keeping your left hand over your heart chakra, slowly raise your right hand up the line of your chakras from the base to the crown. Pause at each chakra until you feel balance at that level. Each chakra is a station where you are processing light.

You can do this last step three or four times. Each time, starting at the base, sense that you are sealing the light and raising the light. You can assist this action by breathing deeply.

Return to the heart

10. To conclude this exercise, bring your right hand back to your heart chakra, placing it on top of your left hand. Chant the sacred syllable *Om* for the sealing of this meditation.

Holistic Approaches
to Healing

Health is the vital principle of bliss.
—JAMES THOMSON

Healing is not something that happens to us. It's something that happens within us. It starts with understanding how our emotional and spiritual health impact our physical vitality—and vice versa. Today many are turning to alternative, or complementary, therapies to create this holistic approach to healing. Many of these therapies apply ancient techniques to our modern circumstances.

Some six hospitals in the United States have departments or clinics that offer innovative complementary care alongside conventional treatments. Perhaps the most well-known is the Program in Integrative Medicine at the University of Arizona, directed by alternative-health guru Dr. Andrew Weil, author of the best-selling *Spontaneous Healing*. His program offers a range of alternative treatments in a hospital setting, including herbal remedies, acupuncture, vitamin therapy, therapeutic touch and prayer.

Holistic therapies facilitate the healing of the whole person—body, mind and spirit—and attempt to stimulate the body's natural healing abilities. They can often help us get to the root of a condition rather than just treating the symptoms. These therapies deal with energy flow and, directly or indirectly, with the body's seven energy centers.

In this section, we review some of the most popular holistic therapies. Please note that they are not intended to replace regular medical diagnosis or to be used as a substitute for proper medical care when it is necessary.

Homeopathy

Homeopathy is a system of medicine developed in the late 1700s and early 1800s by German physician Samuel Hahnemann. It became popular in the United States in the decades after the Civil War. In fact, in 1900 there were twenty-two homeopathic colleges and more than one hundred homeopathic hospitals. About one in every five medical doctors was a homeopath.

The practice of homeopathic medicine declined as modern medicine came on the scene, but since 1980 there has been a resurgence of interest in this healing art in the United States. Several European countries use homeopathy as part of their national health-care systems.

Homeopathy comes from the Greek words meaning "similar" and "suffering" and is based on the principle of "the law of similars," a principle found in Chinese and Indian texts written five thousand years ago and referred to by Hippocrates and Paracelsus. The law of similars states that like cures like. Applied to homeopathy, it means that a substance that will *cause* certain symptoms in a healthy person can *cure* those same symptoms in an unhealthy person when given in minute doses. This is the same principle used in treating allergies with tiny doses of an allergen and including small doses of viruses or bacteria in immunizations to cause the immune system to kick in.

More than two thousand homeopathic remedies have been created from natural substances in the plant, mineral and animal kingdoms. Their manufacture and sale is regulated by the Food and Drug Administration. Unlike most conventional medicine, homeopathic remedies do not try to treat or suppress symptoms. Instead, they go to the root of the problem and stimulate the body to heal itself.

Recognizing that mental and emotional imbalances are reflected in our physical condition, homeopathy addresses not only physical problems, but also the emotional and mental symptoms that accompany them. Homeopathy also works from the premise that each person is unique and that there is a unique remedy for each condition. In diagnosing a condition, a homeopath will ask questions about the patient's mental, emotional and physical condition in order to get an accurate "symptom picture." The correct remedy that matches these symptoms will cause the body to respond and balance itself.

Joyce Waid, a homeopath with over twenty-five years experience, says that as we work with homeopathic remedies, layers of imbalance can be peeled off. "We ideally go deeper and deeper, and become clearer and clearer," she says. "Homeopathy can help us work through and unlock energies that could interfere with the functioning of our chakras and prevent us from expressing our full potential."

As the remedies work over time, she says, conditions resulting from childhood experiences and inherited weaknesses common to our families can be addressed. "The goal is to leave behind the tendencies that hold us back," she says, "and to express more and more of who we are."

Homeopathic remedies are inexpensive and in most cases can be used along with standard medical treatments. Many books and even software can be used for self-care, or you can see an experienced homeopath for a complete program that addresses your needs.

Nourishment and Vitamin Therapy

"An apple a day keeps the doctor away" may have been true in the 1800s, but it's not so today. From the time your food is picked to the time it gets to your dinner plate, it may have lost half to three-quarters of its nutrients.

Fifty years ago, for example, one hundred grams of spinach contained 158 mg of iron. Today, that same amount contains 2.2 mg of iron. The culprits range from nutrient-deficient soil and environmental pollution to the loss of nutrients through drying, storage, hydrogenation, ultrafiltration and irradiation. On top of these factors, many of us can add stress—in the form of emotional pressure, physical overwork and lack of sleep—which virtually eats up our reservoir of vitamins and minerals.

Given statistics like these, many health practitioners have concluded that the average American diet just does not provide the necessary nutrients for good health and that most of us need good nutritional supplementation. Good health through nutrition isn't just about what we eat or don't eat, however. It's also about cleansing and about the way our mind, body and spirit work together.

202

When we look in the mirror and notice problems, we're seeing the outward reflection of inner imbalances, says best-selling author, nutritionist and consultant Ann Louise Gittleman. These are caused not only by lack of good nutrients, but also by toxic overload and mental, emotional or spiritual blocks. "It's more essential than ever before to rid ourselves of these toxins and deal with our physical health so our spiritual life can shine through," says Gittleman. "The right nutrition, internal cleansing, and hormonal harmony are the pathways to attaining natural beauty and vitality."[1]

The seven fundamentals that can help us stay balanced and beautiful, she says, are (1) a cleansed system, (2) purified water, (3) powerful proteins (lean meats and fish rich in omega-3 fatty acids, like salmon and trout, for instance), (4) beautifying oils, (5) energizing and immune-boosting veggies and fruits (fresh, organic and nonstarchy), (6) balanced hormones, and (7) revitalizing vitamins, minerals and antioxidants.

According to Gittleman, detoxing doesn't mean fasting or eating food you've never heard of before. In fact, research is showing that detoxification requires nutritional support so that the liver can do its work. The liver detoxifies and filters everything you ingest, and it is one of the keys to good health. Anything from highly refined foods and preservatives to caffeine, alcohol, smog, second-hand smoke and the Pill can prevent your liver from doing its job.

A sluggish liver can take its toll in other areas of our life. "Unresolved or prolonged anger and depression—the emotional markers of a compromised liver—prevent the body's energy from flowing as it should," says Gittleman.[2] This can result in a wide range of secondary symptoms, such as splitting or breaking fingernails, mood swings, hormonal imbalances, anxiety, mental fogginess, early menopausal symptoms, hot flashes and digestive problems.

In addition to the seven keys to good health named above, Gittleman suggests supporting the liver and all the systems of our body by eating according to the season, a concept based on Traditional Chinese Medicine.[3] She also emphasizes that certain kinds of fat are critical to our health and to the cleansing process because they attract the fat-soluble poisons lodged in fatty tissues of the body and carry them out of the system for elimination. A daily dose of one tablespoon of flaxseed oil, the world's richest source of omega-3 fatty acids, will give you the most bang for your buck, says Gittleman.

She also points out the importance of vitamin B complex for calm nerves and to avoid that washed-out look, zinc to assuage anxiety and promote wound healing and strong hair, vitamin D for calcium absorption and strong bones, and magnesium to encourage tranquility. And last but not least, says Gittleman, "we need to be informed consumers and educate ourselves."

Some healing traditions also encourage us to eat according to where we live. Naturopathic doctor Elisabeth Kirchhof, for instance, advises, "Ask yourself: Could this food grow where I live? The more you eat foods that have a similar energy to where you live, because they too can grow there, the stronger you become physically, spiritually and emotionally."

What effect does our physical condition have on our energy centers? "You can't hold light if you're toxic," says Gittleman. Her years of one-on-one counseling have shown her that when people are detoxifying, they also begin to clean up other areas of their life. "When people have physical clarity, they're much more willing to deal with discomforting or toxic emotions that they have been suppressing. Unspoken words are now able to be spoken," she says. "Internal physical cleansing is a very practical and essential first step to getting spiritual clarity."

Acupuncture

Acupuncture, an ancient Chinese practice, is one of the most popular alternative health treatments today. The World Health Organization says the method can be used to treat more than forty ailments. According to Traditional Chinese Medicine, health and vitality are achieved when there is an abundant flow of energy through the body's meridians. The meridians are the pathways through which our vital energy (qi or ch'i) travels to our organs and our entire body.

An acupuncturist inserts very thin needles at different points along the meridians to increase or decrease the flow of energy to organs that might be weak, thereby restoring balance to the body. As an adjunct to their healing work, acupuncturists may also use herbs and other treatments.

Acupuncture looks at the body, emotions and spirit to get a complete picture of what is needed for healing. "Whenever our emotions are out of balance," says acupuncturist Saskia Peck, "there will be an imbalance in the body as well, and vice versa, because the physical and the emotional cannot be separated. If the body's energetic balance is restored, emotional balance will also be restored."

As with any other healing technique, we have to make adjustments in our lives if the balance that acupuncture brings is to be permanent. "If you are under a lot of stress, you need to look at your life differently so you won't create the same pattern," says Peck. "You may need to adjust your diet so it won't create imbalances in your body. You may need to meditate so you can become more peaceful. You may need to change your emotional responses to the circumstances of your life."

Putting your nature in order is like tuning a stringed instrument.

—WANG CHE

Maintaining a balanced diet, exercising and creating a balanced lifestyle will all contribute to well-being. "Where there is harmony, energy can flow freely," says Peck. "When you are centered, when you are at peace and when your body is strong, your organs and energy centers will be strong too—and you will enjoy physical, emotional and spiritual well-being."

When choosing an acupuncturist, look for one who is certified by the National Certification Commission for Acupuncture and Oriental Medicine.

Herbal Medicine

Herbs have been used since ancient times to heal the body, clear the mind and soothe the soul. The Native American Morning Dove once said, "Everything on earth has a purpose, every disease an herb to cure it, and every person a mission."

Herbs and herbal medicine help strengthen the body's innate healing abilities by cleansing and enhancing our internal environment. The numerous ingredients in herbs work synergistically, and herbs are easily metabolized and utilized by the body.

"As herbs heal our bodies, they can heal our emotions and our minds," says Kirchhof, who has worked with herbs for nearly thirty years. "Herbs can be used to tone, cleanse and rejuvenate the organs associated with the chakras. When burdens in the body are removed, the chakras can experience greater vitality."

Herbs can be taken internally (as tinctures, capsules or teas) and can be applied externally (as ointments or poultices). Everyone can potentially benefit from herbal medicine through self-study, but you may wish to seek professional advice to understand how herbal remedies can complement other therapies you may be using. If you have a serious or long-term health challenge, you will want to consult a health-care professional trained in herbal medicine, such as an herbalist or naturopathic doctor.

Bach Flower Remedies and Flower Essences

Flowers as well as herbs have healing properties. One system of medicine that accesses the healing power of flowers was developed in the 1930s by Dr. Edward Bach, a British physician, bacteriologist and pathologist. Bach came to realize that the underlying cause of illness was emotional imbalance and that healing was more successful when it was treated on the basis of distinctive personality characteristics rather than on the basis of the specific disease.

His thirty-eight Bach Flower Remedies, made from wildflowers and the flowers of wild shrubs, bushes and trees, are taken in minute doses in liquid form. Prescribed on the basis of different emotional tendencies, these remedies work at subtle levels of our being. They help us recognize and work with the inner causes of our outer maladies to bring about internal and external healing.

For Bach, "disease is in essence the result of conflict between Soul and Mind, and will never be eradicated except by spiritual and mental effort." He said disease is a result of deep and long-acting forces and that even if a "material treatment alone is apparently successful, this is nothing more than a temporary relief unless the real cause has been removed."

Kirchhof prescribes the Bach remedies when a patient needs help with an underlying negative emotional outlook. "If we've gotten into a mental or emotional rut and we don't know how to get unstuck, the Bach remedies can help us gently get past it," she says. Gittleman calls the Bach Flower Remedies "psychotherapy in a bottle." One of Bach's most well-known formulas is his remedy for emergencies, called Rescue Remedy. "Rescue Remedy has gotten my clients and me through many stressful situations," says Gittleman, "including car accidents, surgeries, divorce proceedings, courtroom appearances, and just plain everyday anxiety and tension."[4]

Many health food stores carry the Bach Flower Remedies, which you can choose by matching them to your symptoms. New formulas of flower essences are also being developed and are on the market.

Chiropractic

The chiropractic approach to health deals with treating the musculoskeletal system to bring balance to the body's structure and nerve system. Chiropractic comes from the Greek word meaning "effective treatment by hand." Chiropractors adjust the bones and joints, especially the spine, to bring the body back into alignment.

This type of therapy starts from the premise that lack of proper nerve function can cause illness. There are thirty-one pairs of spinal nerves that exit the spine. They comprise an intricate network that affects every tissue of the body. When the spine is in alignment, the nerves can function properly.

Chiropractic also views the body as a self-regulating organism that can heal itself. Both the structure and condition of the body affect how well the body can express its healing potential.

Dr. Merle Bouma, who has practiced chiropractic for thirty-five years, says that while some health practitioners work from a mental, emotional or spiritual approach to bring about physical healing, "chiropractic employs physical means to support spiritual, mental and emotional health."

He says that treating the musculoskeletal system is only the beginning of what a chiropractor does. "When chiropractors treat people," says Bouma, "their hands are actually instruments of healing. The energy in the hands is instrumental in initiating a response from the receptors of the nervous system. Through the hands you are contacting energy centers and reflex centers that impact and help integrate the systems of the body."

212

Aromatherapy

Aromatherapy is a healing art that seeks to improve physical and emotional health using aromatic essential oils taken from nature's own pharmacy. Essential oils have an ancient history and are mentioned in the sacred scriptures of many of the world's religions.

Essential oils are concentrated volatile oils distilled from the roots, stems, leaves, flowers and other elements of a plant. They can be applied in several ways, including through massage, baths, compresses and inhalation.

When the oils are diffused into the air through a diffuser, for instance, the aroma of the plant is conveyed by the olfactory nerve to areas of the brain that can stimulate physical, emotional and mental responses. When used in a massage or bath, the oils, which are absorbed into the skin and carried throughout the body, can affect the entire body within twenty minutes.

Among their many restorative effects, essential oils have been used to relax muscles, stimulate circulation, relieve pain, enhance immunity, alleviate physical, emotional and mental stress, and fight bacteria, infection and fungus. Essential oils are also used in treating environmental sensitivities to neutralize toxins that may be in the air or in the environs, such as in the carpet, walls or ceiling.

Health practitioners, including medical doctors, are beginning to use essential oils to enhance their treatments. In Europe, where there has been more medical research on the use of aromatherapy than in the United States, the use of this healing technique is more common than in the United States. Some European pharmacies even carry essential oils.

Like other integrated healing modalities, aromatherapy supports the body, mind and spirit and helps strengthen the body so it can heal itself. Anna Maya Eisvang, a longtime teacher in the fields of natural health and aromatherapy, says scientific research has shown that essential oils have a high vibrational frequency, varying from approximately 50 MHz to 320 MHz. "Using essential oils helps increase the frequency of the body," she says, "which enhances the body's natural flow of energy through the meridian and chakra systems and increases immunity."

Essential oils are considered to be powerful because they work at cellular levels. "Physical, emotional and mental blockages can prevent the exchange of nutrients within the cells and the release of toxins from the cells," says Eisvang. "Essential oils have properties that cause rejuvenation at the cellular level."

Eisvang says that essential oils are not the same as perfume oils and fragrances, which can contain unnatural chemicals. For an essential oil to have therapeutic quality, the oil needs to be grown organically and carefully harvested and distilled. The oil cannot be cut or diluted with petrochemicals.

An easy way to start using essential oils, says Eisvang, is to take a therapeutic grade A oil that is right for your condition, place one drop in your hand, rub the palms of your hands together, and then hold your palms up to your nose and smell the fragrance. The oils can have a powerful effect and yet evaporate quickly.

Yoga

Yoga was developed in India some five thousand years ago. The word *yoga* means "union," and its aim was union with the divine and with the true self. Apart from its spiritual underpinnings, today yoga is being practiced by thousands to relax, control stress, gain mental clarity and improve physical fitness and health.

Research has shown that yoga can help manage or control anxiety and stress, asthma, back pain, blood pressure, carpal tunnel syndrome, headaches and a variety of other conditions and illnesses. There are many kinds of yoga and they typically include certain postures, breathing exercises and meditation. Yoga can increase strength by toning the muscles. The breathing exercises that accompany some forms of yoga help circulate the universal life-force (prana, or energy) throughout the body, which enhances health and vitality.

> *Energy is
> eternal delight.*
> —WILLIAM BLAKE

Massage

To Hippocrates, the father of Western medicine, massage was an important part of any health regime. In addition to its relaxing effects, scientific research shows that massage has therapeutic and rehabilitative value and can help a wide range of conditions.

Massage helps to eliminate toxins, align bones, muscles and ligaments, and restore the full range of motion to joints. Some forms of massage also aim at freeing energy blocks at deeper levels, stimulating emotional and even spiritual change. In addition, like other holistic techniques, massage promotes health by boosting the body's intrinsic healing abilities.

Massage is especially helpful for those who have bone or muscle injuries or are inactive and subject to stress. Stress can cause our vessels to constrict, which reduces circulation. Massage, in turn, stimulates the nervous system and increases circulation, encouraging the health of our muscles and organs.

In addition, massage greatly increases the flow of lymph, which removes bacteria from the tissues. Lymph primarily moves through our lymphatic vessels when the muscles surrounding the vessels move and contract, creating a massaging effect. When we are inactive, lymph can stagnate.

There are many different styles of massage,

and you should feel free to speak with a massage therapist to be sure he or she offers the right kind of massage for you.

Spa Therapies

Whether it's a short visit to a day spa or a longer time-out at a fancy destination spa far away from home, the spa experience is fast becoming an important part of many people's approach to health care. From ancient times, the spa experience was a natural healing therapy. Today spas offer a variety of treatments, including massage, skin care, hand and foot treatments, body scrubs, body wraps and water therapies.

The treatments that spas offer are more than pampering. They can be de-stressing, replenishing and healing for body, mind and soul. "Certain therapies, like mineral water therapies and the use of seaweeds and mud, can replenish minerals that have been depleted through stress," says Monica Tuma Brown, a spa development consultant and former spa director with a special interest in hydrotherapy.

218

Spa treatments are like nourishing yourself from the outside in, says Brown. "When you eat a good organic salad, you're nourishing yourself inside. You're getting a lot of folic acid, magnesium, vitamins and iron," she says. "If you're in a mineral or mud bath or a seaweed body wrap, the skin absorbs nutrients. It's like wrapping yourself in a good salad."

Brown says water therapies are used in about one quarter of the spas in the United States. The word *spa* is probably derived from the Latin words *sanitas per aquas,* meaning "health through water," and the original spa therapies were always based on the use of water.

Water therapies offered at spas can impact our health in three major ways, says Brown. First, the water will have different effects based on what you put in the water, such as essential oils, oatmeal or baking soda, or what is in the natural mineral springs. Second, our body weight is displaced in water so we have greater mobility in water, which can facilitate healing. Third, hot and cold water have thermal effects that can relax or stimulate. Hydrotherapy has also been shown to help the circulatory, digestive, lymphatic and nervous systems.

Today some spas are becoming a meeting ground for traditional and complementary therapies—a place you can go for a holistic health-care experience. On the third floor of the Philadelphia-based Toppers day spa, for example, the Wellness Sciences Institute employs a variety of practitioners spanning traditional medicine, chiropractic, homeopathy, acupuncture, naturopathic medicine and yoga. The spa staff and the doctors recommend each other's services when visitors need them. This kind of holistic approach is the trend in other spas as well. "We're going to see more and more spas combined with clinics and wellness centers that offer both medical and natural therapies," predicts Brown.

John Fanuzzi, president of Golden Ratio Woodworks, agrees. "In the next ten years, the trend will be the marriage of the spa industry to the medical and alternative healing communities," he says. Fanuzzi, who is also a practitioner of Polarity therapy, is expanding into this territory himself by opening Wellspring Institute in Montana, a combined treatment and training center. Along with its spa therapies, like wet treatments and body wraps with algae and mud, the institute will offer different alternative healing modalities each day of the week.

"People will be able to have a full range of treatments here," says Fanuzzi. In addition, Fanuzzi plans to host conferences, lectures and advanced training on a variety of techniques, such as massage, hydrotherapy, acupuncture, craniosacral treatments, aromatherapy, advanced skin care, and light, color and sound therapies.

"These treatments can work synergistically to bring people to a place of peace so they can have a physical as well as spiritual experience," says Fanuzzi. "It's not just about outer beauty; it's also about inner beauty. My goal is to see everyone home with a life-changing experience."

Just as important as the therapies that spas offer is the "pampering factor"—the fact that we've taken time out for ourselves and recognize the need to nourish both body and soul. "When you allow yourself to take time out apart from this techno-crazy world," says Brown, "the next thing you know you've transported yourself mentally and physically. At spas you find people who love to make other people feel good—which isn't unlike the healthcare industry. It's all about taking care of people. It's all about holistic wellness and connectedness."

Notes

Integrating Body, Mind and Spirit

1. In Jewish mystical tradition, the Tree of Life is composed of ten *sefirot*, or divine emanations, arranged in seven different levels.

2. These are the positions of the seven major energy centers. There are actually a total of 144 energy centers in the body.

3. Lao Tsu, *Tao Te Ching*, trans. Gia-fu Feng and Jane English (New York: Random House, Vintage Books, 1972), chap. 25.

First Energy Center: Base of the Spine

Opening quotation: Brian Walker, *Hua Hu Ching: The Unknown Teachings of Lao Tzu* (HarperSanFrancisco, 1992), no. 50, p. 62.

1. Ramana Maharshi, quoted in Stephen Mitchell, *The Gospel According to Jesus: A New Translation and Guide to His Essential Teachings for Believers and Unbelievers* (New York: HarperCollins Publishers, HarperPerennial, 1991), p. 47.

2. Thomas Moore, *Care of the Soul: A Guide for Cultivating Depth and Sacredness in Everyday Life* (New York: HarperCollins Publishers, 1992), p. 271.

3. Sri Aurobindo, "The Role of Money," *Parabola: The Magazine of Myth and Tradition,* Spring 1991, pp. 10–11.

4. Barry Vissell and Joyce Vissell, *The Shared Heart: Relationship Initiations and Celebrations* (Aptos, Calif.: Ramira Publishing, 1984), pp. 30–31.

5. Kahlil Gibran, *The Prophet* (New York: Alfred A. Knopf, 1923), pp. 15, 16.

Second Energy Center: Seat of the Soul

1. Daniel C. Matt, *The Essential Kabbalah: The Heart of Jewish Mysticism* (HarperSanFrancisco, 1996), p. 127.

2. Gospel of Thomas, logion 2, in James M. Robinson, ed., *The Nag Hammadi Library in English,* 3d ed. (HarperSanFrancisco, 1988), p. 126.

3. See "Removing the Mask," in Mark L. Prophet and Elizabeth Clare Prophet, *The Lost Teachings of Jesus I* (Corwin Springs, Mont.: Summit University Press, 1994), chap. 1.

4. Edward F. Edinger, *Ego and Archetype: Individuation and the Religious Function of the Psyche* (Boston: Shambhala Publications, 1972), p. 103.

Third Energy Center: Solar Plexus

1. *Karma* is a Sanskrit word meaning "act," "action," "word" or "deed." Karma, both positive and negative, is the effect of causes we have set in motion in the past, whether ten minutes ago or ten embodiments ago. Karma is the consequences of our thoughts, words and deeds.

2. James 1:2–4.

3. Walker, *Hua Hu Ching,* no. 36, p. 42.

4. Jack Kornfield and Christina Feldman, eds., *Soul Food: Stories to Nourish the Spirit and the Heart* (HarperSanFrancisco, 1996), pp. 124-25.

Clearing the Energy Centers

Opening quotation: Walker, *Hua Hu Ching,* no. 45, p. 55.

1. For more information on the violet flame and how to apply it to your spiritual practice, see Elizabeth Clare Prophet's *Spiritual Techniques to Heal Body, Mind and Soul* (90-min. audiocassette) and these books in her Pocket Guides to Practical Spirituality series: *Violet Flame to Heal Body, Mind and Soul* and *The Art of Practical Spirituality: How to Bring More Passion, Creativity and Balance into Everyday Life,* published by Summit University Press.

2. Fritjof Capra, *The Tao of Physics,* 2d ed. (New York: Bantam Books, 1984), p. 141.

3. The "Chakra Affirmations" and other violet-flame

prayers and affirmations are included on *Spiritual Techniques to Heal Body, Mind and Soul* (see note 1 above).

Fourth Energy Center: Heart

1. Coleman Barks et al., *The Essential Rumi* (HarperSanFrancisco, 1995), p. 92.

2. Ibid., p. 109.

3. Doc Childre and Howard Martin, with Donna Beech, *The HeartMath Solution* (HarperSanFrancisco, 1999), pp. 37-38.

4. Thomas Cleary, trans. and ed., *Vitality, Energy, Spirit: A Taoist Sourcebook* (Boston: Shambhala Publications, 1991), p. 233.

5. Thomas Merton, *Thoughts in Solitude* (Boston: Shambhala Publications, Shambhala Pocket Classics, 1993), p. 58.

6. Wing-tsit Chan, trans., *The Way of Lao Tzu (Tao-te ching)* (Indianapolis, Ind.: Bobbs-Merrill Company, 1963), chap. 78, p. 236.

7. Robert G. Henricks, trans., *Lao-tzu: Te-Tao Ching* (New York: Ballantine Books, 1989), chap. 43, p. 108.

8. Cheng Man-ch'ing, *Master Cheng's Thirteen Chapters on T'ai-Chi Ch'üan,* trans. Douglas Wile (Brooklyn, N.Y.: Sweet Ch'i Press, 1982), p. 7.

Fifth Energy Center: Throat

1. Christmas Humphreys, ed., *The Wisdom of Buddhism* (London: Curzon Press, 1987), pp. 67–68.

2. C. W. Leadbeater, *The Masters and the Path*, 3d ed., abr. (Adyar, Madras: Theosophical Publishing House, 1969), pp. 86, 87.

3. Ibid., p. 87.

4. See William J. Bennett, ed., *The Book of Virtues: A Treasury of Great Moral Stories* (New York: Simon & Schuster, 1993), pp. 74–78.

5. Lao Tsu, *Tao Te Ching*, trans. Feng and English, chaps. 56, 52.

6. Humphreys, *The Wisdom of the Buddha*, p. 68.

7. Ibid., p. 67.

8. Thomas Cleary, trans., *The Essential Confucius: The Heart of Confucius' Teachings in Authentic I Ching Order* (HarperSanFrancisco, 1992), p. 27.

9. Stephen R. Covey, *The Seven Habits of Highly Effective People: Restoring the Character Ethic* (New York: Simon & Schuster, 1989), pp. 134-35.

10. Exod. 3:13–15.

Sixth Energy Center: Third Eye

1. Kuthumi and Djwal Kul, *The Human Aura: How to Activate and Energize Your Aura and Chakras*

(Corwin Springs, Mont.: Summit University Press, 1996), pp. 262, 266.

2. Matt, *The Essential Kabbalah*, p. 116.

3. Napoleon Hill, *Think and Grow Rich*, rev. ed. (New York: Ballantine Books, Fawcett Crest Book, 1960), pp. 179, 181.

4. See Elizabeth Clare Prophet and Mark L. Prophet, *Creative Abundance: Keys to Spiritual and Material Prosperity* (Corwin Springs, Mont.: Summit University Press, 1998), p. 96.

5. Aung San Suu Kyi with Alan Clements, *The Voice of Hope* (New York: Seven Stories Press, 1997), pp. 52, 53.

6. Ibid., p. 114.

7. Ibid., pp. 157–58.

Seventh Energy Center: Crown

1. Hill, *Think and Grow Rich*, p. 178.

2. Kornfield and Feldman, *Soul Food*, p. 351.

3. Marion L. Matics, trans., *Entering the Path of Enlightenment: The* Bodhicaryavatara *of the Buddhist Poet Santideva* (London: George Allen & Unwin, 1971), pp. 162, 163.

4. Merton, *Thoughts in Solitude*, pp. 141–42.

5. Ibid., p. 136.

6. Katha Upanishad, quoted in Bede Griffiths, *Universal Wisdom: A Journey through the Sacred Wisdom of the World* (London: HarperCollins Publishers, Fount, 1994), pp. 57, 60, 62.

Holistic Approaches to Healing

1. Ann Louise Gittleman, interview, January 16, 2000; and Ann Louise Gittleman, *The Living Beauty Detox Program: The Revolutionary Diet for Each and Every Season of a Woman's Life* (HarperSanFrancisco, 2000), p. 2.

2. Gittleman, *The Living Beauty Detox Program*, p. 32.

3. See *The Living Beauty Detox Program*, pp. 49–107.

4. Gittleman, *The Living Beauty Detox Program*, p. 151.

Alchemy of the Heart

"There is no way you can read this book and not feel more love for those around you—and as you do, you can see the healing changes that love will bring." MAGICAL BLEND MAGAZINE

"Through this 'pocket guide to practical spirituality' we learn the alchemical means to heal and empower our hearts, fulfill our reason for being, and extend our capacity to love. In other words, we learn how we can become 'a living transformer of love.'" BODHI TREE BOOK REVIEW

ISBN: 0-922729-60-3
204 pages $6.95

Karma and Reincarnation

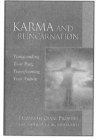

The word *karma* has made it into the mainstream. But not everyone understands what it really means or how to deal with it. This insightful book will help you come to grips with karmic connections from past lives that have helped create the circumstances of your life today. You'll discover how your actions in past lives affect which family you're born into, who you're attracted to, and why some people put you on edge. And you'll learn how to turn your karmic encounters into grand opportunities to shape the future you want.

ISBN: 0-922729-61-1
224 pages $6.95

ISBN: 0-922729-48-4
165 pages $5.95

Soul Mates and Twin Flames

"After thirty-five years as a relationship counselor, I find *Soul Mates and Twin Flames* to be extremely powerful in revealing the inner mysteries of the soul and the true essence of love through its insightful analysis of real-life experiences and classical love stories."

MARILYN C. BARRICK, Ph.D.,
author of *Sacred Psychology of Love*

ISBN: 0-922729-41-7
118 pages $5.95

How to Work with Angels

"Angels—and our relationship to them—are neither a trend nor a fad....Ultimately, one's relationship with an angel is a personal one, and in *How to Work with Angels*, you'll discover how to make angels more present in your life....
Whether for love, healing, protection, guidance, or illumination, angels stand ready to help you in many practical and personal ways....Also included here are a collection of visualizations, affirmations, prayers and decrees."

BODHI TREE BOOK REVIEW

Creative Abundance

"*Creative Abundance* contains keys for magnetizing the spiritual and material abundance we all need. Its sensible step-by-step techniques—including treasure mapping, principles of feng shui, meditations, visualizations and affirmations—show how to live a full and prosperous life."

BODHI TREE BOOK REVIEW

ISBN: 0-922729-38-7
173 pages $5.95

Violet Flame to Heal Body, Mind & Soul

"The violet flame is a light that serves all spiritual heritages, that gives respect and dignity to all things. It gives us a way to connect with each other....It's what really empowers you."

DANNION BRINKLEY,
author of *Saved by the Light*

ISBN: 0-922729-37-9
108 pages $5.95

Edgar Cayce recognized the healing power of the violet light. Dannion Brinkley saw and experienced the violet flame in his near-death sojourns. Healers and alchemists have used this high-frequency spiritual energy to bring about energetic balance and spiritual transformation. Now you can apply the practical techniques in this book to create balance, harmony and positive change—in body, mind and soul.

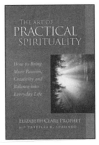

ISBN: 0-922729-55-7
154 pages $5.95

The Art of Practical Spirituality

Create your own intimate relationship with Spirit and learn how to bring more passion, creativity and balance into everyday life. This commonsense guide offers practical steps for staying in tune with Spirit midst the hustle and bustle of everyday life. For listening to the still small voice within. For living in the here and now. And it gives creative techniques we can use to uplift ourselves and the world around us.

POCKET GUIDES TO PRACTICAL SPIRITUALITY audiobooks:

Alchemy of the Heart
The Art of Practical Spirituality
Creative Abundance
Karma and Reincarnation
Soul Mates and Twin Flames
Your Seven Energy Centers

Summit University Press books are available at fine bookstores worldwide and at your favorite on-line bookseller. Our books have been translated into 20 languages and are sold in more than 30 markets worldwide. If you would like a free catalog of our books and products, please contact

Summit University Press, PO Box 5000, Corwin Springs, MT 59030-5000 USA. Tel: 1-800-245-5445 or 406-848-9500. Fax: 1-800-221-8307 or 406-848-9555. E-mail: info@summituniversitypress.com
www.summituniversitypress.com

WHAT CAN WE EXPECT THROUGH 2025?

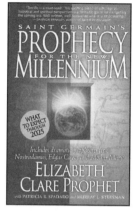

*"Terrific—
a must-read!*
*This exciting blend of astro-
logical, historical and
spiritual perspectives is a
fantastic guide for navigating
the coming era. Well written,
well researched and very
empowering."*

—DANNION BRINKLEY,
author of *Saved by the Light*

*Saint Germain's Prophecy
for the New Millennium*
explores the most compelling

ISBN 0-922729-45-X
pocketbook   394 pages $7.99

prophecies for our time from Nostradamus, Edgar
Cayce, Mother Mary and Saint Germain. And it
introduces a high-frequency spiritual energy that
can help us create the future we want.

*"Elizabeth Clare Prophet reminds us that by
our heartfelt connection with Spirit, in deed and
thought, we can bring about the staying of the
hand of darkness and bring on an Aquarian age
of unprecedented light."*

—JESS STEARN, author of *Edgar Cayce on the Millennium*

SUMMIT UNIVERSITY ⟲ PRESS

Spiritual Techniques to Heal Body, Mind and Soul

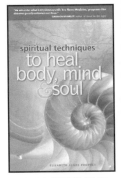

"As we enter what Larry Dossey calls 'Era Three medicine,' programs like this one greatly enhance our lives. ...Allows a deeper connectiveness and understanding of how, in a fast-paced world, we can maintain spiritual cohesiveness. I recommend this tape for the novice, avid seeker and advanced student."

—DANNION BRINKLEY,
author of *Saved by the Light*

ISBN: 0-922729-59-X
90-min. audiocassette
$10.95

Elizabeth Clare Prophet, bestselling author and pioneer in practical spirituality, explores dynamic techniques for using the creative power of sound to transform our personal lives and bring spiritual solutions to today's global challenges.

Learn how to combine visualization, affirmation and meditation to fulfill greater levels of your own inner potential. Shows how to access a high-frequency spiritual energy to improve relationships, increase mental clarity and energize the body's seven energy centers. Includes research from well-known experts on the science of mantra.

SUMMIT UNIVERSITY PRESS
To order call 1-800-245-5445